# 20 THINGS
# YOU SHOULD READ

compiled by:
david edwards ▪ margaret feinberg
janella griggs ▪ matthew paul turner

Tyndale House Publishers, Inc.
Carol Stream, Illinois

Library of Congress Cataloging-in-Publication Data
Twenty things you should read / by David Edwards ... [et al.].
  p. cm.
  ISBN-13: 978-1-4143-0595-0 (sc)
  ISBN-10: 1-4143-0595-8 (sc)
  1. Christian life. I. Edwards, David, date.
BV4495.T84 2006
230--dc22                                              2005027067

Printed in the United States of America

12  11  10  09  08  07  06

7   6   5   4   3   2   1

# TABLE OF CONTENTS

Consider a scene from the movie *Dead Poets Society*. Robin Williams's character, John Keating, tells the boys in his class to look at the pictures of former students. Most of these men were probably dead, but Keating doesn't care. He says to the boys, "If you listen real close, you can hear them whisper their legacy to you.... Go on, lean in. Listen....Hear it?" And then Keating whispers, "Carpe diem." His voice gets a little bit louder. "CARPE DIEM." Then he whispers again, "Seize the day."

Among the film's many great scenes, that one in particular stands out. Why? Because it validates the lives of those men who are now gone. Keating obviously wants his students to appreciate the lives of the men who had once walked the school's grounds. They have lessons to share with his class.

That's why we love this book, *Twenty Things You Should Read*. It brings value to names, faces, stories, and words of those from the past who walked through this Christian life with passion, mystique, and wisdom. These twenty men and women you're about to meet were selected from a long list of those who have gone before us because of their contributions through their writings, lives, and places in history.

Much of their language is far removed from modern-day lingo. That's why we've added all kinds of clues to help you understand the text. Brief introductions, historical facts, and comments throughout will help you navigate the sometimes unfamiliar and difficult wording.

They'll also illustrate the uncanny relevance of the subject matter for today's generation.

Sure, these men and women lived in different circumstances than what we experience today. But their love for Jesus and God's Word was strong, controversial, and unwavering. Reading the passionate words of these spiritual giants is challenging and inspiring.

There's something about looking back to the past that brings more meaning to the present and more hope for the future. You'll likely find yourself amazed by how much you can relate to the themes these great thinkers wrote about.

It's in the writings these individuals left behind that we find the essence of their faith. Whether they walked through hard times of sickness or imprisonment or the death of a child, their confidence in our good God remained. Their faith wasn't perfect; they didn't have flawless theology, but they all had compelling stories. And it was in those true-life struggles and triumphs that their voices rose to the surface of their times.

What can reading the classics do for you? Since the beginning of time, humankind has struggled to know God. We know this, yet there's often a crazy tendency to think we're the only one on earth struggling with doubt, questioning tradition, or yearning for intimacy with God. We hide our true vulnerability so our image or worth isn't threatened by feeling somehow different from everyone else. Reading the classics reminds us that we're not so different.

We're not so alone.

There's *freedom* when we read the vulnerable, passionate words of men and women who lived hundreds of years ago and yet struggled with many of the same issues.

There's *beauty* in the eloquent, deliberate writing styles of the past. The poetry and literary prowess are inspiring.

There's *hope* when we read the honest struggles and realize these long-gone authors sought God and found him.

There's *inspiration* when we read about godly men and women in lifelong pursuits of their Savior.

God's message of love and salvation hasn't changed throughout the generations. These excerpts are testimonies to his faithful plans, his eternal plans—his plans that *work* for life, no matter when or where we live.

It's our prayer that this book communicates Christ's timeless, unrelenting love for you and his desire to be the center of your own personal faith journey. You're part of an eternal plan with a powerful purpose. You're part of something bigger than yourself. We hope you'll be inspired to question, explore, and grow. We hope you'll be motivated to make your lives count in such a way that, years from now, others will be impacted by your passion the way we're moved by these authors from yesterday.

It's our hope that when you read these writings, you'll think about the man or woman behind the words. Listen to what they had to say to the audiences of their times. And let their wisdom seep into your soul.

*Dave Edwards,*
*Margaret Feinberg,*
*Janella Griggs,*
*Matthew Paul Turner*

# VITAL STATS

**WHEN AND WHERE:** Aurelius Augustinus lived in a small town in North Africa and partied like a rock star before his conversion to Christianity.

**STYLE:** Augustine is candid and convincing in his presentation. He is regretful about his past but confident of his future and faith in God.

**NOTEWORTHY ACCOMPLISHMENT:** He is considered one of the founders of Western theology. Augustine's influence on Christianity is considered by some to be second only to the apostle Paul.

**TIMELESS WISDOM:** Augustine's story teaches us that no one is beyond redemption and that God will go to great lengths to pursue someone—even in the midst of their own rebellion.

Almost everyone had given up on Aurelius. He was rebellious and belligerent, and he had a natural tendency to hang out with the wrong crowd. Despite his mother's religious devotion, Aurelius chose a promiscuous, unruly lifestyle. By the age of eighteen, he had fathered a child, but rather than marry the woman, he kept her as a mistress.

As Aurelius entered his twenties, his life didn't change. He began writing a bit, but the majority of his time was spent debating academic issues in theater-related activities. In many regards, Aurelius was about as far away from God as you could get. Yet his mother, a praying woman, refused to give up on him. She beat heaven's gates in prayer, until one day Aurelius woke up from the drunken stupor of his life. He came to faith in Jesus and dedicated his life to the priesthood.

Aurelius eventually became the bishop of the North African city of Hippo, and today he's simply known as Saint Augustine. Though his life was confined to the fourth and fifth centuries, his influence has been felt for more than a millennium. His book, *Confessions*, provides a moving account of one soul's journey toward grace. It recounts the story of his childhood, youth, and conversion to Christianity at the age of thirty-two. What makes Aurelius's story so unusual is its timelessness. It's the classic sinner-turned-saint story, yet it's so much more. It's honest and unapologetic in its prose. In the excerpt below, St. Augustine reflects on his sixteenth year—one of his rebellious years—with regret and remorse. The amazing testimony of his life and legacy is that no one is beyond redemption.

*Margaret*

# ST. AUGUSTINE
Excerpted from *Confessions*[1]

## BOOK TWO, CHAPTER I
*Looking Back*

I wish now to review in memory my past wickedness and the carnal corruptions of my soul—not because I still love them, but that I may love thee, O my God. For love of thy love I do this, recalling in the bitterness of self-examination my wicked ways, that thou mayest grow sweet to me, thou sweetness without deception! Thou sweetness happy and assured! Thus thou mayest gather me up out of those fragments in which I was torn to pieces, while I turned away from thee, O Unity, and lost myself among "the many." For as I became a youth, I longed to be satisfied with worldly things, and I dared to grow wild in a succession of various and shadowy loves. My form wasted away, and I became corrupt in thy eyes, yet I was still pleasing to my own eyes—and eager to please the eyes of men.

## CHAPTER II

But what was it that delighted me save to love and to be loved? Still I did not keep the moderate way of the love of mind to mind—the bright path of friendship. Instead, the mists of passion steamed up out of the puddly concupiscence of the flesh, and the hot imagination of puberty, and they so obscured and overcast my heart that I was unable to distinguish pure affection from unholy desire. Both boiled confusedly within me, and dragged my unstable youth down over the cliffs of unchaste desires and plunged me into a gulf of infamy. Thy anger had come upon me, and I knew it not. I had been deafened by the clanking of the chains of my mortality, the punishment for my soul's pride, and I wandered farther from thee, and thou didst permit me to do so. I was tossed to and fro, and wasted, and poured

> Augustine is honest but regretful about his youthful, rebellious ways.

out, and I boiled over in my fornications—and yet thou didst hold thy peace, O my tardy Joy! Thou didst still hold thy peace, and I wandered still farther from thee into more and yet more barren fields of sorrow, in proud dejection and restless lassitude.

If only there had been someone to regulate my disorder and turn to my profit the fleeting beauties of the things around me, and to fix a bound to their sweetness, so that the tides of my youth might have spent themselves upon the shore of marriage! Then they might have been tranquilized and satisfied with having children, as thy law prescribes, O Lord—O thou who dost form the offspring of our death and art able also with a tender hand to blunt the thorns which were excluded from thy paradise!

Augustine recognizes just how far he got from God.

For thy omnipotence is not far from us even when we are far from thee. Now, on the other hand, I might have given more vigilant heed to the voice from the clouds: "Nevertheless, such shall have trouble in the flesh, but I spare you," and, "It is good for a man not to touch a woman," and, "He that is unmarried cares for the things that belong to the Lord, how he may please the Lord; but he that is married cares for the things that are of the world, how he may please his wife." I should have listened more attentively to these words, and, thus having been "made a eunuch for the Kingdom of Heaven's sake," I would have with greater happiness expected thy embraces.

It's amazing to see how Augustine recognizes God's presence even in the midst of his wild days.

But, fool that I was, I foamed in my wickedness as the sea and, forsaking thee, followed the rushing of my own tide, and burst out of all thy bounds. But I did not escape thy scourges. For what mortal can do so? Thou wast always by me, mercifully angry and flavoring all my unlawful pleasures with bitter discontent, in order that I might seek pleasures free from discontent. But where could I find such pleasure save in thee, O Lord—save in thee, who dost teach us by sorrow, who woundest us to heal us, and dost kill us that we may not die apart from thee. Where was I, and how far was I exiled from the delights of thy house, in that sixteenth year of the age of my flesh, when the madness of lust held full sway in me—that madness which grants indulgence to human shamelessness, even though it is forbidden by thy laws—and I gave myself entirely to it? Meanwhile, my family took no care to save me from ruin by marriage, for their sole care was that I should learn how to make a powerful speech and become a persuasive orator. . . .

From the sound of this next paragraph, Augustine never really expected to be widely read, let alone have one of the biggest influences on the history of Christianity.

## CHAPTER III

To whom am I narrating all this? Not to thee, O my God, but to my own kind in thy presence—to that small part of the human race who may chance to come upon these writings. And to what end? That I and all who read them may understand what depths there are from which we are to cry unto thee. For what is more surely heard in thy ear than a confessing heart and a faithful life? . . .

During that sixteenth year of my age, I lived with my parents, having a holiday from school for a time—this idleness imposed upon me by my parents' straitened finances. The thornbushes of lust grew rank about my head, and there was no hand to root them out. Indeed, when my father saw me one day at the baths and perceived that I was becoming a man, and was showing the signs of adolescence, he joyfully told my mother about it as if already looking forward to grandchildren, rejoicing in that sort of inebriation in which the world so often forgets thee, its Creator, and falls in love with thy creature instead of thee—the inebriation of that invisible wine of a perverted will which turns and bows down to infamy. But in my mother's breast thou hadst already begun to build thy temple and the foundation of thy holy habitation—whereas my father was only a catechumen, and that but recently. She was, therefore, startled with a holy fear and trembling: for

Despite the fact that his mother pulled him aside and told him not to sleep around—especially with married women—Augustine refused to listen and reveled in pushing the envelope.

Augustine's years as a twentysomething were filled with regrets over giving in to the typical temptations we all face. However, those worldy lures eventually lost their appeal and left him empty. His life ultimately was marked by great success because he discovered a relationship with his Savior that far surpassed any of the world's temporary thrills.

though I had not yet been baptized, she feared those crooked ways in which they walk who turn their backs to thee and not their faces.

### God Was There All Along

Woe is me! Do I dare affirm that thou didst hold thy peace, O my God, while I wandered farther away from thee? Didst thou really then hold thy peace? Then whose words were they but thine which by my mother, thy faithful handmaid, thou didst pour into my ears? None of them, however, sank into my heart to make me do anything. She deplored and, as I remember, warned me privately with great solicitude, "not to commit fornication; but above all things never to defile another man's wife." These appeared to me but womanish counsels, which I would have blushed to obey.

Yet they were from thee, and I knew it not. I thought that thou wast silent and that it was only she who spoke. Yet it was through her that thou didst not keep silence toward me; and in rejecting her counsel I was rejecting thee—I, her son, "the son of thy handmaid, thy servant." But I did not realize this, and rushed on headlong with such blindness that, among my friends, I was ashamed to be less shameless than they, when I heard them boasting of their disgraceful exploits—yes, and glorying all the more the worse their baseness was. What is worse, I took pleasure in such exploits, not for the pleasure's sake only but mostly for praise. What is worthy of vituperation except vice itself? Yet I made myself out worse than I was, in order that I might not go lacking for praise. And when in anything I had not sinned as the worst ones in the group, I would still say that I had done what I had not done, in order not to appear contemptible because I was more innocent than they; and not to drop in their esteem because I was more chaste.

# VITAL STATS

**WHEN AND WHERE:** Julian of Norwich lived during a time when the bubonic plague swept through England multiple times, so she was familiar with pain and suffering.

**STYLE:** Considered one of the great mystics, Julian uses colorful language to express divine love.

**NOTEWORTHY ACCOMPLISHMENT:** Her book, *Revelations of Divine Love*, is one of the first books ever written by an English woman.

**TIMELESS WISDOM:** Julian had a contagious passion to know the depths of God, no matter what the price.

Julian of Norwich comes from a land I scarely know. Born in the fourteenth century, she lived as a mystic—something that seems so foreign and aged and odd to the rational American world we live in today. Her relationship with God was very real to her, and she experienced him through divine visions and revelations.

Historians suspect she was a Benedictine nun. When she was thirty years old, she became ill to the point of death. Seven days later, after the medical crisis was over, Julian had a series of sixteen visions, or "showings," of Jesus in which she felt led to embrace and reflect upon the passion of Christ. After her health was fully restored, Julian lived in a small hut near a church in Norwich. For the next twenty years, she reflected on her visions through contemplation and prayer. She recorded her insights in a book called *Revelations of Divine Love*, one of the first books written in English by a woman.

The writing—which at times seems consumed with death—is saturated with the life of Christ. Considering her surroundings, it isn't surprising that Julian focused on death so much. She grew up watching the bubonic plague sweep through her village and country. The deaths of friends, relatives, and neighbors were inevitable.

She had experienced loss, but she had also experienced something much more powerful—the all-embracing life of Christ that permeated her soul with hope and love. It is in this context that Julian prayed one of the bravest prayers in history. She begged God to give her three gifts.

First, she wanted to grasp the reality of Christ's final hours to understand not only Jesus' physical pains but also the compassion of those who witnessed his persecution. Second, she asked for a sickness to come upon her at the age of thirty so that she could experience death without actually dying. She believed this would help purge her and allow her to live all the more for God. Finally, she asked for three internal wounds: true contrition, natural compassion, and an unshakable longing for God.

It seems all three of these requests were answered in Julian's "showings," and the flavor of those desires infuses *Revelations of Divine Love*. At times the old English is hard to understand, but if you'll suffer through the rougher portions, you'll discover an unmistakably contagious desire for God—to know him and to be known by him. While Julian's mystical experiences are worthy of theological discussion and debate, the impact of the visions on Julian's understanding of God's love are without question. How can one who has suffered so much still know the richness of God's love? That question is one of the great Christian paradoxes.

May God give you a revelation of his divine love as you reflect on the writings of Julian of Norwich.

*Margaret*

# JULIAN OF NORWICH
Excerpted from *Revelations of Divine Love*[2]

## CHAPTER II

These Revelations were shewed to a simple creature unlettered, the year of our Lord 1373, the
Thirteenth day of May. Which creature [had]
afore desired three gifts of God. The First was
mind of His Passion; the Second was bodily sickness in youth, at thirty
years of age; the Third was to have of God's gift three wounds.

*Julian makes three rather unusual requests of God.*

As to the First, methought I had some feeling in the Passion of Christ,
but yet I desired more by the grace of God. Methought I would have been
that time with Mary Magdalene, and with other that were Christ's lovers,
and therefore I desired a bodily sight wherein I might have more knowledge
of the bodily pains of our Saviour and of the compassion of our Lady and of
all His true lovers that saw, that time, His pains. For I would be one of them
and suffer with Him. Other sight nor shewing of God desired I never none,
till the soul were disparted from the body. The
cause of this petition was that after the shewing I
should have the more true mind in the Passion of
Christ.

The Second came to my mind with contrition;
[I] freely desiring that sickness [to be] so hard as
to death, that I might in that sickness receive all
my rites of Holy Church, myself thinking that I
should die, and that all creatures might suppose
the same that saw me: for I would have no manner of comfort of earthly life. In this sickness I desired to have all manner of pains bodily and
ghostly that I should have if I should die, (with all the dreads and tempests
of the fiends) except the outpassing of the soul. And this I meant for [that] I

*Julian wanted to encounter the passion of the Christ where she could understand not only the bodily pains of Jesus but also the compassion that emerges through suffering.*

would be purged, by the mercy of God, and afterward live more to the worship of God because of that sickness. And that for the more furthering in my death: for I desired to be soon with my God.

These two desires of the Passion and the sickness I desired with a condition, saying thus: *Lord, Thou knowest what I would,—if it be Thy will that I have it—; and if it be not Thy will, good Lord, be not displeased: for I will nought but as Thou wilt.*

Julian asked for a physical sickness to come upon her to help purge her so she could live all the more for God. Talk about a strange and dangerous prayer!

For the Third [petition], by the grace of God and teaching of Holy Church I conceived a mighty desire to receive three wounds in my life: that is to say, the wound of very contrition, the wound of kind compassion, and the wound of steadfast longing toward God. And all this last petition I asked without any condition.

These two desires aforesaid passed from my mind, but the third dwelled with me continually.

## CHAPTER III
### When Sickness Comes

In other words, Julian wanted a heart that was softened with true contrition, natural compassion, and an unshakable longing for God.

And when I was thirty years old and a half, God sent me a bodily sickness, in which I lay three days and three nights; and on the fourth night I took all my rites of Holy Church, and weened not to have lived till day. And after this I languored forth two days and two nights, and on the third night I weened oftentimes to have passed; and so weened they that were with me.

And being in youth as yet, I thought it great sorrow to die;—but for nothing that was in earth that me liked to live for, nor for no pain that I had fear of: for I trusted in God of His mercy. But it was to have lived that I might have loved God better, and longer time, that I might have the more knowing and loving of God in bliss of Heaven. For

methought all the time that I had lived here so little and so short in regard of that endless bliss,—I
thought [it was as] nothing. Wherefore I thought:
*Good Lord, may my living no longer be to Thy wor-*
*ship!* And I understood by my reason and by my
feeling of my pains that I should die; and I as-
sented fully with all the will of my heart to be at
God's will.

As strange of a
prayer as Julian
prayed (to become
sick), she got what
she asked for!

Thus I dured till day, and by then my body was
dead from the middle downwards, as to my feeling. Then was I minded to be set upright, back-
ward leaning, with help,—for to have more
freedom of my heart to be at God's will, and
thinking on God while my life would last.

My Curate was sent for to be at my ending,
and by that time when he came I had set my eyes,
and might not speak. He set the Cross before my
face and said: *I have brought thee the Image of thy*
*Master and Saviour: look thereupon and comfort*
*thee therewith.*

The word *methought*
means just what it
sounds like—"me
thought" or "I
thought.". . . Cool,
huh? Maybe we can
convince Webster to
add it back into the
dictionary.

Methought I was well [as it was], for my eyes were set uprightward unto
Heaven, where I trusted to come by the mercy of God; but nevertheless I as-
sented to set my eyes on the face of the Crucifix, if I might; and so I did. For
methought I might longer dure to look evenforth than right up.

After this my sight began to fail, and it was all dark about me in the
chamber, as if it had been night, save in the Image of the Cross whereon I
beheld a common light; and I wist not how. All that was away from the
Cross was of horror to me, as if it had been greatly occupied by the fiends.

After this the upper part of my body began to die, so far forth that
scarcely I had any feeling;—with shortness of breath. And then I weened in
sooth to have passed.

And in this [moment] suddenly all my pain was taken from me, and I was as whole (and specially in the upper part of my body) as ever I was afore.

I marvelled at this sudden change; for methought it was a privy working of God, and not of nature. And yet by the feeling of this ease I trusted never the more to live; nor was the feeling of this ease any full ease unto me: for methought I had liefer have been delivered from this world.

> Julian thought she was going to die, but she was revived. In the midst of such pain and suffering, her heart was still focused on God.

Then came suddenly to my mind that I should desire the second wound of our Lord's gracious gift: that my body might be fulfilled with mind and feeling of His blessed Passion. For I would that His pains were my pains, with compassion and afterward longing to God. But in this I desired never bodily sight nor shewing of God, but compassion such as a kind soul might have with our Lord Jesus, that for love would be a mortal man: and therefore I desired to suffer with Him.

## CHAPTER V
### A Deeper Understanding

In this same time our Lord shewed me a spiritual sight of His homely loving. I saw that He is to us everything that is good and comfortable for us: He is our clothing that for love wrappeth us, claspeth us, and all encloseth us for tender love, that He may never leave us; being to us all-thing that is good, as to mine understanding.

> Julian was able to learn of creation's dependence on God's loving nature from a hazelnut.

Also in this He shewed me a little thing, the quantity of an hazel-nut, in the palm of my hand; and it was as round as a ball. I looked thereupon with eye of my understanding, and thought: *What may this be?* And it was answered generally thus: *It is all that is made.* I marvelled how it might last, for methought it might suddenly have fallen to naught for little[ness]. And I was answered in my understanding: *It lasteth, and ever shall [last] for that God loveth it.* And so All-thing hath the Being by the love of God.

In this Little Thing I saw three properties. The first is that God made it, the second is that God loveth it, the third, that God keepeth it. But what is to me verily the Maker, the Keeper, and the Lover,—I cannot tell; for till I am Substantially oned to Him, I may never have full rest nor very bliss: that is to say, till I be so fastened to Him, that there is right nought that is made betwixt my God and me.

> The lesson of the hazelnut remains true today. God not only made you, but he loves you, and he promises to keep you.

It needeth us to have knowing of the littleness of creatures and to hold as nought all-thing that is made, for to love and have God that is unmade. For this is the cause why we be not all in ease of heart and soul: that we seek here rest in those things that are so little, wherein is no rest, and know not our God that is All-mighty, All-wise, All-good. For He is the Very Rest. God willeth to be known, and it pleaseth Him that we rest in Him; for all that is beneath Him sufficeth not us. And this is the cause why that no soul is rested till it is made nought as to all things that are made. When it is willingly made nought, for love, to have Him that is all, then is it able to receive spiritual rest.

Also our Lord God shewed that it is full great pleasance to Him that a helpless soul come to Him simply and plainly and homely. For this is the natural yearnings of the soul, by the touching of the Holy Ghost (as by the understanding that I have in this Shewing): *God, of Thy Goodness, give me Thyself: for Thou art enough to me, and I may nothing ask that is less that may be full worship to Thee; and if I ask anything that is less, ever me wanteth,— but only in Thee I have all.*

And these words are full lovely to the soul, and full near touch they the will of God and His Goodness. For His Goodness comprehendeth all His creatures and all His blessed works, and overpasseth without end. For He is the endlessness, and He hath made us only to Himself, and restored us by

Doeth thouth under-standeth alleth the wordeths that endeth with *th*? If not, cut the *th* off and they'll make more sense(th)!

His blessed Passion, and keepeth us in His blessed love; and all this of His Goodness.

# VITAL STATS

**WHEN AND WHERE:** Thomas à Kempis was born in Kempen in the Prussian Rhine province north of Cologne. His influence was important to the continued growth and expansion of the church and Christian literature during the fifteenth century.

**STYLE:** His quiet style and demeanor did not bring Thomas à Kempis widespread notoriety during his life, but it did earn him respect from his peers inside the church and from many outside the church who knew and admired his faithful lifestyle.

**NOTEWORTHY ACCOMPLISHMENTS:** Thomas à Kempis was a scribe and copied the entire Bible four times. His book, *The Imitation of Christ*, has been a must-read for centuries.

**TIMELESS WISDOM:** "In all things I sought quiet and found it not save in retirement and in books." Thomas à Kempis lived a very simple and humble life, but his influential habits of simplicity and holiness touched everyone around him and still provide a wise example for modern twentys to imitate.

Wealth. Power. Fame. They—and their appeal—are as old as human nature. If we're honest, who wouldn't like a taste of each one? We enter adulthood full of dreams and goals for a successful life, admirable ambitions in and of themselves. But many souls waste precious years striving down paths that appear to lead to fulfillment, all the while missing out on the truly lasting priorities. In the end they're left with empty promises and hollow lives. It's possible few people have successfully risen above these temptations as well as Thomas à Kempis.

From his early years, à Kempis observed the illusion riches present to the average person, but he was somehow able to make the connection that a person's character mattered more than the size of his or her bank account.

Born into a working-class family whose last name meant "Little Hammer," à Kempis knew about hard work.

THOMAS À KEMPIS 1379 OR 1380–1471

He modeled his life after the simplicity and humility he observed in the life Christ exhibited in Scripture and committed to live what he calls the "dying life" as Jesus described in Luke 9:23-24: "If any of you wants to be my follower, you must turn from your selfish ways, take up your cross daily, and follow me. . . . If you give up your life for my sake, you will save it."

Humans haven't really changed much over the centuries. In our society, as in both Jesus' and à Kempis's, it's easy to forget the importance of living for something larger than yourself. Many of the influences we face encourage us to focus only on fulfilling our own wishes and desires. Thomas à Kempis reminds us that God created life to be larger and fuller than we can ever hope to understand. But the life focused on self is doomed to smallness and serious limitations. The life lived in the pursuit of giving itself away for God and others will always find the fullness and abundance Christ himself promised.

There are few human accolades to à Kempis's credit, but his life and writings show us that the entrance to heaven has a low door frame—we can only enter submissively on our knees. He tells us the arrogant will soon forget to stay on their knees, but they'll be reminded by the bumps on the head as they try to stand up in their own self-worth.

The following excerpt comes from his book, *The Imitation of Christ.* This updated version stays faithful to the original tone with wording that appeals to today's readers. The gentle yet powerful text reveals the secrets behind the serious pursuit of the dying life.

By the year 1900, *The Imitation of Christ* had been published in over six thousand editions; that's more than one per month for five hundred years. It has been called the most published of all books other than the Bible.

For over five hundred years, this tender book has provided inspiration to millions of readers in over fifty languages, and still serves as a powerful example of passionate living for what really matters.

*Dave*

# THOMAS À KEMPIS
Excerpted from *The Imitation of Christ*[3]

## BOOK II, CHAPTER 12
### *Living for God Includes Suffering*

To many the saying, "Deny thyself, take up thy cross and follow Me," seems hard, but it will be much harder to hear that final word: "Depart from Me, ye cursed, into everlasting fire." Those who hear the word of the cross and follow it willingly now, need not fear that they will hear of eternal damnation on the day of judgment. This sign of the cross will be in the heavens when the Lord comes to judge. Then all the servants of the cross, who during life made themselves one with the Crucified, will draw near with great trust to Christ, the judge.

Why, then, do you fear to take up the cross when through it you can win a kingdom? In the cross is salvation, in the cross is life, in the cross is protection from enemies, in the cross is infusion of heavenly sweetness, in the cross is strength of mind, in the cross is joy of spirit, in the cross is highest virtue, in the cross is perfect holiness. There is no salvation of soul nor hope of everlasting life but in the cross.

Take up your cross, therefore, and follow Jesus, and you shall enter eternal life. He Himself opened the way before you in carrying His cross, and upon it He died for you, that you, too, might take up your cross and long to die upon it. If you die with Him, you shall also live with Him, and if you share His suffering, you shall also share His glory.

Behold, in the cross is everything, and upon your dying on the cross

Thomas à Kempis dives right into this section, which actually appears in Book Two of *The Imitation of Christ*. If you're feeling lost, read on! He's simply writing about living for Jesus above everything else, which includes being willing to suffer losses in this world for God's higher purposes in eternity.

everything depends. There is no other way to life and to true inward peace than the way of the holy cross and daily mortification. Go where you will, seek what you will, you will not find a higher way, nor a less exalted but safer way, than the way of the holy cross. Arrange and order everything to suit your will and judgment, and still you will find that some suffering must always be borne, willingly or unwillingly, and thus you will always find the cross.

Either you will experience bodily pain or you will undergo tribulation of spirit in your soul. At times you will be forsaken by God, at times troubled by those about you and, what is worse, you will often grow weary of yourself. You cannot escape, you cannot be relieved by any remedy or comfort but must bear with it as long as God wills. For He wishes you to learn to bear trial without consolation, to submit yourself wholly to Him that you may become more humble through suffering.

No one understands the passion of Christ so thoroughly or heartily as the man whose lot it is to suffer the like himself.

There's a purpose to our suffering. We become more humble, like Jesus, when we patiently endure the tough circumstances God allows in our lives. There's comfort in that truth. Imagine what a waste it would be to live through troubles for nothing!

The cross, therefore, is always ready; it awaits you everywhere. No matter where you may go, you cannot escape it, for wherever you go you take yourself with you and shall always find yourself. Turn where you will—above, below, without, or within—you will find a cross in everything, and everywhere you must have patience if you would have peace within and merit an eternal crown.

If you carry the cross willingly, it will carry and lead you to the desired goal where indeed there shall be no more suffering, but here there shall be. If you carry it unwillingly, you create a burden for yourself and increase the load, though still you have to bear it. If you cast away one cross, you will find another and perhaps a heavier one. Do you expect to escape what no mortal man can ever avoid? Which of the saints was without a cross or trial on this earth? Not even Jesus Christ, our Lord, Whose every hour on earth knew the pain of His passion. "It behooveth Christ to suffer, and to rise again from the dead, . . . and so enter into his glory." How is it that you look for another way than this, the royal way of the holy cross?

The whole life of Christ was a cross and a martyrdom, and do you seek rest and enjoyment for yourself? You deceive yourself, you are mistaken if you seek anything but to suffer, for this mortal life is full of miseries and marked with crosses on all sides. Indeed, the more spiritual progress a person makes, so much heavier will he frequently find the cross, because as his love increases, the pain of his exile also increases.

### A Greater Hope Comes through Suffering

Yet such a man, though afflicted in many ways, is not without hope of consolation, because he knows that great reward is coming to him for bearing his cross. And when he carries it willingly, every pang of tribulation is changed into hope of solace from God. Besides, the more the flesh is distressed by affliction, so much the more is the spirit strengthened by inward grace. Not infrequently a man is so strengthened by his love of trials and hardship in his desire to conform to the cross of Christ, that he does not wish to be without sorrow or pain, since he believes he will be the more acceptable to God if he is able to endure more and more grievous things for His sake.

It is the grace of Christ, and not the virtue of man, which can and does bring it about that through fervor of spirit frail flesh learns to love and to gain what it naturally hates and shuns.

To carry the cross, to love the cross, to chastise the body and bring it to

What hope à Kempis brings to his readers! After hitting us with the reality that Christ's followers will not be exempt from pain, he points our attention to the greater comfort and strength we can experience as we get to know God better.

subjection, to flee honors, to endure contempt gladly, to despise self and wish to be despised, to suffer any adversity and loss, to desire no prosperous days on earth—this is not man's way. If you rely upon yourself, you can do none of these things, but if you trust in the Lord, strength will be given you from heaven and the world and the flesh will be made subject to your word. You will not even fear your enemy, the devil, if you are armed with faith and signed with the cross of Christ.

We've got to rely on Christ's help if we're going to be truly successful in the Christian life.

Set yourself, then, like a good and faithful servant of Christ, to bear bravely the cross of your Lord, Who out of love was crucified for you. Be ready to suffer many adversities and many kinds of trouble in this miserable life, for troublesome and miserable life will always be, no matter where you are; and so you will find it wherever you may hide. Thus it must be; and there is no way to evade the trials and sorrows of life but to bear them.

Drink the chalice of the Lord with affection if you wish to be His friend and to have part with Him. Leave consolation to God; let Him do as most pleases Him. On your part, be ready to bear sufferings and consider them the greatest consolation, for even though you alone were to undergo them all, the sufferings of this life are not worthy to be compared with the glory to come.

When you shall have come to the point where suffering is sweet and acceptable for the sake of Christ, then consider yourself fortunate, for you have found paradise on earth. But as long as suffering irks you and you seek to escape, so long will you be unfortunate, and the tribulation you seek to evade will follow you everywhere. If you put your mind to the things you ought to consider, that is, to suffering and death, you would soon be in a better state and would find peace.

Although you were taken to the third heaven with Paul, you were not thereby insured against suffering. Jesus said: "I will show him how great things he must suffer for My name's sake." To suffer, then, remains your lot, if you mean to love Jesus and serve Him forever.

If you were but worthy to suffer something for the name of Jesus, what great glory would be in store for you, what great joy to all the saints of God, what great edification to those about you! For all men praise patience though there are few who wish to practice it.

With good reason, then, ought you to be willing to suffer a little for Christ since many suffer much more for the world.

Realize that you must lead a dying life; the more a man dies to himself, the more he begins to live unto God.

No man is fit to enjoy heaven unless he has resigned himself to suffer hardship for Christ. Nothing is more acceptable to God, nothing more helpful for you on this earth than to suffer willingly for Christ. If you had to make a choice, you ought to wish rather to suffer for Christ than to enjoy many consolations, for thus you would be more like Christ and more like all the saints. Our merit and progress consist not in many pleasures and comforts but rather in enduring great afflictions and sufferings.

If, indeed, there were anything better or more useful for man's salvation than suffering, Christ would have shown it by word and example. But He clearly exhorts the disciples who follow Him and all who wish to follow Him to carry the cross, saying: "If any man will come after Me, let him deny himself, and take up his cross daily, and follow Me."

When, therefore, we have read and searched all that has been written, let this be the final conclusion—that through much suffering we must enter into the kingdom of God.

# VITAL STATS

**WHEN AND WHERE:** Martin Luther spent his most influential years near Wittenberg, Germany, during the papacy of Pope Leo X, widely regarded as the most corrupt church official of the age. Tension was mounting worldwide during this time of transition from the Middle Ages to the Modern Ages.

**STYLE:** A timid young monk, Luther was a humble man with no intention of causing a ruckus. He spent his growing-up years being terrified of God's wrath and feeling incapable of earning God's favor. When he discovered the "true Gospel" of the Scripture, his countenance, demeanor, and passion evolved beyond timidity to unmatched fervor. He could not help but rock the tradition-laden corruption in the church.

**NOTEWORTHY ACCOMPLISHMENTS:** Known as the "Father of the Reformation," Luther is one of only a handful of people who have truly changed the course of human history. The Reformation is said to have officially begun with the nailing of his Ninety-five Theses to the door of the Wittenberg Church. He is also known for translating the Bible into German, which made a significant contribution toward uniformity in that language. He also penned numerous songs, including "A Mighty Fortress Is Our God."

**TIMELESS WISDOM:** We're saved by faith alone, not by our own good works or religious acts. Nothing can be done to *earn* salvation, for it is only attained through faith in Jesus Christ. Neither tradition nor religion nor culture can be trusted as absolute truth—only the perfect, infallible Word of God! (So we should probably read and study it as much as possible in our quest for truth.)

Martin Luther is one of the most influential rebels in history. His defiant choice to attend seminary at age twenty-two instead of going to law school, like his dad wanted, turned out to be a good one. Let's hear it for all of us who narrowly missed law school by a fraction of an ounce of our own volition! Later, his revolt against the corrupt Catholic Church of

**MARTIN LUTHER** 1483–1546

the sixteenth century was the tipping point that led to a new era in Christianity and the Protestant Reformation.

Throughout his twenties, Luther was plagued with doubts and guilt. He was an ideal student and a brilliant scholar, however, and he was honored with an assignment in Rome. The plan backfired, though, because instead of settling down and finding peace, he found religious ethics that make Enron and Martha look like Girl Scouts. While he was there, he saw firsthand the extent of corruption and irreverence in the church. He was outraged over the misappropriation of funds and the selling of indulgences with the false promise that people could buy salvation. The experience planted a seed for the now-famous Ninety-five Theses, the list of grievances that he nailed to the door of the church in Wittenberg, Germany, on October 31, 1517.

Through the years of struggle that followed, Luther poured himself into the study of Scripture like never before. He was convinced that the true, infallible Word of God was the only source he could trust for truth. (See? I told you he was a really smart guy!) He became more and more interested in the practical and theological workings of salvation through Christ.

Meanwhile, another contemporary of his, philosopher Desiderius Erasmus, was trying to clean out the moral corruption in the Catholic Church too. Many people assumed the two outspoken men would unite in their efforts, but Luther and Erasmus could not join forces because they were worlds apart on several critical issues. Two of the biggest issues were (1) our free will to choose God vs. God's election of us and (2) the inerrancy and clarity of Scripture. Both of those were nonnegotiables for Luther.

Erasmus wrote a treatise outlining his views, calling it *Discussion Concerning Free Will*. Luther dissected it and refuted just about every sentence in his very lengthy, self-proclaimed masterpiece, *The Bondage of the Will*. And even without the law degree, he cross-examined Erasmus voraciously.

In the excerpts below, notice the passion and conviction exhibited by this once-tormented youth. It's easy to see that he had truly experienced a real encounter with the Author of the Book he loved so much.

You might need to think carefully to absorb it all, but maybe reading his magnum opus will at the very least help confirm that you really weren't supposed to go to law school—and even better, perhaps it will inspire you to develop a burning-hot passion for God's Word like Luther had.

*Janella*

## MARTIN LUTHER
Excerpted from *The Bondage of the Will*[4]

## ERASMUS' SCEPTICISM:
### SECTION 2

What say you, Erasmus? Is it not enough that you submit your opinion to the Scriptures? Do you submit it to the decrees of the church also? What can the church decree, that is not decreed in the Scriptures? If it can, where then remains the liberty and power of judging those who make the decrees? As Paul, [1 Corinthians 14] teaches "Let others judge." Are you not pleased that there should be any one to judge the decrees of the church, which, nevertheless, Paul enjoins? What new kind of religion and humility is this, that, by our own example, you would take away from us the power of judging the decrees of men, and give it unto men without judgment? Where does the Scripture of God command us to do this? . . .

> This sounds a lot like today's popular debate over tolerance. Remember, Jesus wasn't at all concerned with being politically correct or keeping the peace at the expense of truth. In fact, his teachings were quite offensive to many!

In a word, these declarations of yours amount to this—that, with you, it matters not what is believed by any one, any where, if the peace of the world be but undisturbed; and if every one be but allowed, when his life, his reputation, or his interest is at stake, to do as he did, who said, "If they affirm, I affirm, if they deny, I deny:" and to look upon the Christian doctrines as nothing better than the opinions of philosophers and men: and that it is the greatest of folly to quarrel about, contend for, and assert them, as nothing can arise therefrom but contention, and the disturbance of the public peace: "that what is above us, does not concern us."

## SECTION 3

### *The Scriptures Point to Christ As Our Only Savior*

But, that there are in the Scriptures some things abstruse, and that all things are not quite plain, is a report spread abroad by the impious Sophists by whose mouth you speak here, Erasmus. But they never have produced, nor ever can produce, one article whereby to prove this their madness. And it is with such scare-crows that Satan has frightened away men from reading the Sacred Writings, and has rendered the Holy Scripture contemptible, that he might cause his poisons of philosophy to prevail in the church.

This indeed I confess, that there are many *places* in the Scriptures obscure and abstruse; not from the majesty of the thing, but from our ignorance of certain terms and grammatical particulars; but which do not prevent a knowledge of all the *things* in the Scriptures. For what *thing* of more importance can remain hidden in the Scriptures, now that the seals are broken, the stone rolled from the door of the sepulcher, and that greatest of all mysteries brought to light, Christ made man: that God is Trinity and Unity: that Christ suffered for us, and will reign to all eternity? Are not these things known and proclaimed even in our streets? *Take Christ out of the Scriptures, and what will you find remaining in them?*

> Luther says without Christ in the Bible, what else is there? A good point, especially when there is a false belief in much of the world today that "we all worship the same God." The God of Scripture is three-in-one: the Father, Son, and Holy Spirit. He is either all three, or the Bible is a lie.

## SECTION 6

### *Salvation Comes through Faith in Christ, Not by Good Behavior*

The "Form" of Christianity set forth by you, among other things, has this—"That we should strive with all our powers, have recourse to the remedy of repentance, and in all ways try to gain the mercy of God; without which, neither human will, nor endeavour, is effectual." Also, "that no one should despair of pardon from a God by nature most merciful."

These statements of yours are without Christ, without the Spirit, and more cold than ice: so that, the beauty of your eloquence is really deformed by them. Perhaps a fear of the Popes and those tyrants, extorted them from you their miserable vassal, lest you should appear to them a perfect atheist. But what they assert is this—That there is ability in us; that there is a striving with all our powers; that there is mercy in God; that there are ways of gaining that mercy; that there is a God, by nature just, and most merciful, &c.— But if a man does not know what these powers are; what they can do, or in what they are to be passive; what their efficacy, or what their inefficacy is; what can such an one do? What will you set him about doing?

> In this section, Luther addresses the issue of salvation through Jesus, not because of some supposed goodness in us. How could we ever possibly know if we're good enough? It would be like having one final exam that determines whether you pass or fail, but all semester the teacher refuses to teach a class, assign a reading, or even tell you what course you're taking. You can't possibly expect to pass. What are you supposed to do?

## THE NECESSITY OF KNOWING GOD AND HIS POWER
### SECTION 7
*Luther Clarifies Our Works and God's Grace*
Therefore, it is not irreligious, curious, or superfluous, but essentially wholesome and necessary, for a Christian to know, whether or not the will does any thing in those things which pertain unto Salvation. Nay, let me tell you, this is the very hinge upon which our discussion turns. It is the very heart of our subject. For our object is this: to inquire what "Free-will" can do, in what it is passive, and how it stands with reference to the grace of God. *If we know nothing of these things, we shall know nothing whatever of Christian matters, and shall be far behind all People upon the earth.* He

that does not feel this, let him confess that he is no Christian. And he that despises and laughs at it, let him know that he is the Christian's greatest enemy. For, if I know not how much I can do myself, how far my ability extends, and what I can do God-wards; I shall be equally uncertain and ignorant how much God is to do, how far His ability is to extend, and what He is to do toward me: whereas it is "God that worketh all in all." [1 Cor. 12:6.] But if I know not the distinction between our working and the power of God, I know not God Himself.

And if I know not God, I cannot worship Him, praise Him, give Him thanks, nor serve Him; for I shall not know how much I ought to ascribe unto myself, and how much unto God. It is necessary, therefore, to hold the most certain distinction, between the power of God and our power, the working of God and our working, if we would live in His fear.

## THE SOVEREIGNTY OF GOD
### SECTION 9
*God's Will Is Perfect and Trustworthy, Even When We Don't Fully Understand It*
This therefore, is also essentially necessary and wholesome for Christians to know: *That God foreknows nothing by contingency, but that He foresees, purposes, and does all things according to His immutable, eternal, and infallible will.* By this thunderbolt, "Free-will" is thrown prostrate, and utterly dashed to pieces. Those, therefore, who

This is the heart of the matter in Luther's argument with Erasmus and the Catholic Church of the day. His passionate belief in the Scripture's clarity that a person is saved through faith and not by works rings out over and over like a refrain throughout his writings.

For the next few sections, his discussion shifts focus a little. He has established the importance and authority of Scripture, and now he turns toward the argument over free will and election. This fierce debate continues among believers to this day: Do we choose God, or did he choose certain ones to be his?

would assert "Free-will," must either deny this thunderbolt, or pretend not to see it, or push it from them.

## SECTION 24

These things, therefore, are openly proclaimed for the sake of the Elect: that, being by these means humbled and brought down to nothing, they might be saved. The rest resist this humiliation; nay, they condemn the teaching of self-desperation; they wish to have left a little something that they may do themselves. These secretly remain proud, and adversaries to the grace of God. This, I say, is one reason—that those who fear God, being humbled, might know, call upon, and receive the grace of God. . . .

After stating a careful (and lengthy!) case for election and asserting that free will, as propagated by Erasmus, is a prideful, haughty claim to salvation by works, Luther addresses another point of contention—that Scripture is unclear and confusing to the reader. If it was clear to him then, we have no excuse today. He didn't even have the New Living Translation, the NIV, *The Message*, or any of our other modern versions!

This is the highest degree of faith—to believe that He is merciful, who saves so few and damns so many; to believe Him just, who according to His own will, makes us necessarily damnable, that He may seem, as Erasmus says, 'to delight in the torments of the miserable, and to be an object of hatred rather than of love.' If, therefore, I could by any means comprehend how that same God can be merciful and just, who carries the appearance of so much wrath and iniquity, there would be no need of faith.

## SECTION 26
### *Luther Argues That God Has Free Will, We Don't*

It now then follows, that Free-will is plainly a divine term, and can be applicable to none but the divine Majesty only: for He alone "doth, (as the Psalm sings) what He will in Heaven and earth."

[Psalm 135:6] Whereas, if it be ascribed unto men, it is not more properly ascribed, than the divinity of God Himself would be ascribed unto them: which would be the greatest of all sacrilege. Wherefore, it becomes Theologians to refrain from the use of this term altogether, whenever they wish to speak of human ability, and to leave it to be applied to God only. And moreover, to take this same term out of the mouths and speech of men; and thus to assert, as it were, for their God, that which belongs to His own sacred and holy Name.

## EXORDIUM

### SECTION 35

### *Luther Accuses the Church and Defends the Clarity and Reliability of Scripture*

But, since we have been persuaded to the contrary of this, by that pestilent saying of the Sophists, 'the Scriptures are obscure and ambiguous;' we are compelled, first of all, to prove that first grand principle of ours, by which all other things are to be proved: which, among the Sophists, is considered absurd and impossible to be done. . . .

But, let us proceed, and drown that pestilent saying of the Sophists, in Scriptures.

[Psalm 19:8], saith, "The commandment of the Lord is clear (or pure), enlightening the eyes." And surely, that which enlightens the eyes, cannot be obscure or ambiguous!

Again, [Psalm 119:130] "The door of thy words giveth light; it giveth understanding to the simple." Here, it is ascribed unto the words of God, that they are a door, and something open, which is quite plain to all and enlightens even the simple. . . .

> Luther practices what he preaches here by examining Scripture in depth to prove his point. How did he know all these verses? Because he had a lifelong habit of daily studying the Bible.

In [Malachi 2:7], commands, 'that they should seek the law from the mouth of the priest, as being the messenger of the Lord of Hosts.' But a

Whenever anyone, no matter how spiritual or respected, claims the Spirit has told them something, it is our duty to determine the accuracy of their statement based on the Word of God. The Spirit will never tell someone to do something that is contrary to the written Word of God.

most excellent messenger indeed of the Lord of Hosts he must be, who should bring forth those things, which were both so ambiguous to himself and so obscure to the people, that neither he should know what he himself said, nor they what they heard!

## SECTION 36
### *The New Testament Provides More Evidence for Scripture's Truth*

Now let us come to the New Testament. Paul saith, [Romans 1:2,] that the Gospel was promised "by the Prophets in the Holy Scriptures." And, [Romans 3:21,] that the righteousness of faith was testified "by the law and the Prophets."

But what testimony is that, if it be obscure? Paul, however, throughout all his epistles makes the Gospel, the word of light, the Gospel of clearness; and he professedly and most copiously sets it forth as being so, [2 Corinthians 3–4]. . . .

Peter also saith, [2 Peter 1:19,] "And we certainly have more surely the word of prophecy; unto which, ye do well that ye take heed, as unto a light shining in a dark place." Here Peter makes the Word of God a clear lamp, and all other things darkness: whereas, we make obscurity and darkness of the Word. . . .

In a word, if the Scripture be obscure or ambiguous, what need was there for its being sent down from heaven? Are we not obscure and ambiguous enough in ourselves, without an increase of it by obscurity, ambiguity, and darkness being sent down unto us from heaven? And if this be the case, what will become of that of the apostle, "All Scripture is given by inspiration of God, and is profitable for doctrine, for reproof, for correction?" [2 Timothy 3:16] . . . And Christ must also, of necessity, revoke His word where He falsely promises us, saying, "I will give you a mouth and wisdom which all your adversaries shall not be able to re-sist," [Luke 21:15]. For how shall they not resist when we fight against them with obscurities and uncertainties? And why do you also, Erasmus, prescribe to us a form of Christianity, if the Scriptures be obscure to you!

Luther certainly did his homework before defending the absolute truth of the Bible and Jesus as the only way to salvation. He set for us a great example of the courage it takes to stand strong as a Christian in our world—especially when it comes to questioning all those modern religions people flock to today.

# VITAL STATS

**WHEN AND WHERE:** John Calvin was born in France in the early part of the sixteenth century. He was born into Catholicism, but by his mid-twenties, Martin Luther's teachings had turned him Protestant.

**STYLE:** Calvin was dogmatic in his ways and teachings. Because of his angst toward the Catholic Church, many of his views created riots and elicited waves of anti-Protestant sentiment.

**NOTEWORTHY ACCOMPLISHMENT:** Calvin's five highly debated teachings (commonly referred to as TULIP) are the foundation for many reformed churches around the world. In a nutshell, these points deal with (1) the total depravity of man (humankind's sinful nature); (2) unconditional election (our inability to choose God without his first choosing us); (3) limited atonement (Jesus' death provided salvation only for those God chose); (4) irresistible grace (grace is a gift that can't be refused); and (5) perseverance of the saints (true believers will keep their faith forever).

**TIMELESS WISDOM:** "Is it faith to understand nothing, and merely submit your convictions implicitly to the Church?" Regardless of whether you share all of Calvin's views, his life shows the importance of taking responsibility for our own discovery of the Bible's truth.

When I was a junior at Belmont University in Nashville, I went to a Bible study hosted by a local Presbyterian congregation. A young, vibrant minister-in-training stood in front of a group of fifty spiritually eager twentysomethings and discoursed at length about the differences between being considered theologically Arminian or Calvinist. Despite my long history in Christianity, I had never heard of either of these terms. Nor had I ever considered myself to be defined by them. The young preacher, who seemed quite proud of his ponytail, thick-rimmed glasses, and strangely translated Bible (it was the NASV), explained with ease the five main points of Calvinism—it was obvious what side of the theological coin he favored.

Hearing this cool hippie wax philosophical about complicated Christianese concepts like predestination, limited atonement, and irresistible grace sent my unchallenged faith into a tailspin. Sitting there listening to him ramble on about God choosing to save some but not others got me so upset that I left the room in tears. I walked into the bathroom and sobbed over the very idea that God would ever make a choice to send someone to eternal punishment in hell. But apparently, that is what John Calvin believed—in fact, his five-point belief system became a reformation of sorts during his time. I left the event that evening knowing I had to learn more about this character named Calvin.

Calvin lived for fifty-five years during the sixteenth century. He was known as an even greater reformer of the Catholic Church than Martin Luther. His beliefs were controversial, strict, and sweeping. He didn't believe in the separation of church and state—on the contrary, he believed that leaders of the church should also be on the governing board of a town or city. It was his embracing of this type of belief system that got him thrown out of the city of Geneva, only to be invited back a few years later. Surprisingly, Calvin's rigid way of life became popular across Europe in the mid-1500s.

Many believe Calvin's rules of governing helped define America's core values on politics, government, and leadership. Although Calvin's ideas continue to be somewhat controversial nearly 450 years after his death, he is a historical character whom all Christians should know something about.

It was during Calvin's excommunication that he finished *Institutes of the Christian Religion*, his thick commentary on the Bible. Below is an excerpt from chapter 9, entitled "Of Meditating on the Future Life." Read for yourself his thoughts on heaven, death, and the soul. His style is deep, complicated, and intellectual, and his writing moves from point to point, with very few stories and a very King James Version tone. If you'll work through the *eths* and *ists*, you'll discover a work both convicting, powerful, and timeless in its focus on the hope Christians have for life after death.

*Matthew*

# JOHN CALVIN
Excerpted from *Institutes of the Christian Religion*[5]

## BOOK THIRD, CHAPTER 9
### Hard Times Focus Us on Heaven
The principal use of the cross is, that it in various ways accustoms us to despise the present, and excites us to aspire to the future life. In withdrawing from the present life we must neither shun it nor feel hatred for it; but desiring the future life, gladly quit the present at the command of our sovereign Master. Our infirmity in dreading death described.

> The first sentence of point number one is invigorating to our faith. Calvin's cry is that everything good and bad points us to focus more on heaven. A core belief of Calvin's is that nothing can be gained by investing in the things of this world.

1. Whatever be the kind of tribulation with which we are afflicted, we should always consider the end of it to be, that we may be trained to despise the present, and thereby stimulated to aspire to the future life. For since God well knows how strongly we are inclined by nature to a slavish love of this world, in order to prevent us from clinging too strongly to it, he employs the fittest reason for calling us back, and shaking off our lethargy. Every one of us, indeed, would be thought to aspire and aim at heavenly immortality during the whole course of his life. For we would be ashamed in no respect to excel the lower animals; whose condition would not be at all inferior to ours, had we not a hope of immortality beyond the grave. But when you attend to the plans, wishes, and actions of each, you see nothing in them but the earth. Hence our stupidity; our minds being dazzled with the glare of wealth, power, and honors, that they can see no farther. The heart also, engrossed with avarice, ambition, and lust, is weighed down and cannot rise above them. In short, the whole soul, ensnared by the allurements of the flesh, seeks its happiness on the earth. To meet this dis-

ease, the Lord makes his people sensible of the vanity of the present life, by a constant proof of its miseries. Thus, that they may not promise themselves deep and lasting peace in it, he often allows them to be assailed by war, tumult, or rapine, or to be disturbed by other injuries. That they may not long with too much eagerness after fleeting and fading riches, or rest in those which they already possess, he reduces them to want, or, at least, restricts them to a moderate allowance, at one time by exile, at another by sterility, at another by fire, or by other means. That they may not indulge too complacently in the advantages of married life, he either vexes them by the misconduct of their partners, or humbles them by the wickedness of their children, or afflicts them by bereavement. But if in all these he is indulgent to them, lest they should either swell with vainglory, or be elated with confidence, by diseases and dangers he sets palpably before them how unstable and evanescent are all the advantages competent to mortals. We duly profit by the discipline of the cross, when we learn that this life, estimated in itself, is restless, troubled, in numberless ways wretched, and plainly in no respect happy; that what are estimated its blessings are uncertain, fleeting, vain, and vitiated by a great admixture of evil.

2. For there is no medium between the two things: the earth must either be worthless in our estimation, or keep us enslaved by an intemperate love of it. Therefore, if we have any regard to eternity, we must carefully strive to disencumber ourselves of these fetters.

Moreover, since the present life has many enticements to allure us, and great semblance of delight, grace, and sweetness to soothe us, it is of great consequence to us to be now and then called off from its fascinations. For what, pray, would happen, if we here enjoyed an uninterrupted course of honor and felicity, when even the constant stimulus of affliction cannot arouse

*Calvin makes it pretty clear that humanity either loves the world or looks beyond it toward the eternal.*

us to a due sense of our misery? That human life is like smoke or a shadow, is not only known to the learned; there is not a more trite proverb among the vulgar. Considering it a fact most useful to be known, they have recommended it in many well-known expressions. Still there is no fact which we ponder less carefully, or less frequently remember. For we form all our plans just as if we had fixed our immortality on the earth. If we see a funeral, or walk among graves, as the image of death is then present to the eye, I admit we philosophise admirably on the vanity of life. We do not indeed always do so, for those things often have no effect upon us at all. But, at the best, our philosophy is momentary. It vanishes as soon as we turn our back, and leaves not the vestige of remembrance behind; in short, it passes away, just like the applause of a theatre at some pleasant spectacle. Forgetful not only of death, but also of mortality itself, as if no rumor of it had ever reached us, we indulge in supine security as expecting a terrestrial immortality.

We're so easily distracted! All the "allurements" we enjoy about life on earth can distract us from a greater priority. With characteristic logic, Calvin continues to build his argument for our need to focus on eternity.

### God's Earthly Blessings Point Us to Him

3. Still the contempt which believers should train themselves to feel for the present life, must not be of a kind to beget hatred of it or ingratitude to God. This life, though abounding in all kinds of wretchedness, is justly classed among divine blessings which are not to be despised. Wherefore, if we do not recognize the kindness of God in it, we are chargeable with no little ingratitude towards him. To believers, especially, it ought to be a proof of divine benevolence, since it is wholly destined to promote their salvation. Before openly exhibiting the inheritance of eternal glory, God is pleased to manifest himself to us as a Father by minor proofs, . . . and the blessings which he daily bestows upon us. Therefore, while this life serves to acquaint us with the goodness of God, shall we disdain it as if it did not contain one particle of good? We ought, therefore, to feel and be affected towards it in such a manner as to place it among those gifts of the divine benignity which are by

no means to be despised. Were there no proofs in Scripture, (they are most numerous and clear) yet nature herself exhorts us to return thanks to God for having brought us forth into light, granted us the use of it, and bestowed upon us all the means necessary for its preservation.

### Death without the Hope of Heaven Leads to Despair

4. In proportion as this improper love diminishes, our desire of a better life should increase. I confess, indeed, that a most accurate opinion was formed by those who thought, that the best thing was not to be born, the next best to die early. For, being destitute of the light of God and of true religion, what could they see in it that was not of dire and evil omen? Nor was it unreasonable for those who felt sorrow and shed tears at the birth of their kindred, to keep holiday at their deaths. But this they did without profit; because, devoid of the true doctrine of faith, they saw not how that which in itself is neither happy nor desirable turns to the advantage of the righteous: and hence their opinion issued in despair.

Let believers, then, in forming an estimate of this mortal life, and perceiving that in itself it is nothing but misery, make it their aim to exert themselves with greater alacrity, and less hindrance, in aspiring to the future and eternal life.

When we contrast the two, the former may not only be securely neglected, but, in comparison of the latter, be disdained and contemned. If heaven is our country, what can the earth be but a place of exile? If departure from the world is entrance into life, what is the world but a sepulchre, and what is residence in it but immersion in death? If to be freed from the body is to gain full possession of freedom, what is the body but a prison? If it is the very summit of happiness to enjoy the presence of God, is it not miserable to want it? But

In Calvin's view, if we focus on heaven (while still appreciating God's goodness on earth), we are igniting our love for what God has planned for his children. He believes that is why people who don't know Jesus as Savior love this life. They love it because they have nothing to look forward to.

"whilst we are at home in the body, we are absent from the Lord." Thus when the earthly is compared with the heavenly life, it may undoubtedly be despised and trampled under foot. We ought never, indeed, to regard it with hatred, except in so far as it keeps us subject to sin; and even this hatred ought not to be directed against life itself. At all events, we must stand so affected towards it in regard to weariness or hatred as, while longing for its termination, to be ready at the Lord's will to continue in it, keeping far from everything like murmuring and impatience.

### No Fear of Death for Christians!

5. But, most strange to say, many who boast of being Christians, instead of thus longing for death, are so afraid of it that they tremble at the very mention of it as a thing ominous and dreadful. We cannot wonder, indeed, that our natural feelings should be somewhat shocked at the mention of our dissolution. But it is altogether intolerable that the light of piety should not be so powerful in a Christian breast as with greater consolation to overcome and suppress that fear. For if we reflect that this our tabernacle, unstable, defective, corruptible, fading, pining, and putrid, is dissolved, in order that it may forthwith be renewed in sure, perfect, incorruptible, in fine, in heavenly glory, will not faith compel us eagerly to desire what nature dreads?

In this section, Calvin acknowledges that, while it may be natural for Christians to fear death to some degree, our hope of the better life to come should bring great comfort.

If we reflect that by death we are recalled from exile to inhabit our native country, a heavenly country, shall this give us no comfort? But everything longs for permanent existence. I admit this, and therefore contend that we ought to look to future immortality, where we may obtain that fixed condition, which nowhere appears on the earth.

### Our Endurance on Earth Makes Us Like Jesus

6. The whole body of the faithful, so long as they live on the earth, must be

like sheep for the slaughter, in order that they may be conformed to Christ their head. Most deplorable, therefore, would their situation be did they not, by raising their mind to heaven, become superior to all that is in the world, and rise above the present aspect of affairs. On the other hand, when once they have raised their head above all earthly objects, though they see the wicked flourishing in wealth and honor, and enjoying profound peace, indulging in luxury and splendour, and revelling in all kinds of delights, though they should moreover be wickedly assailed by them, suffer insult from their pride, be robbed by their avarice, or as- sailed by any other passion, they will have no dif- ficulty in bearing up under these evils. They will turn their eye to that day, on which the Lord will receive his faithful servants, wipe away all tears from their eyes, clothe them in a robe of glory and joy, feed them with the ineffable sweetness of his pleasures, exalt them to share with him in his greatness; in fine, admit them to a participation in his happiness. But the wicked who may have flourished on the earth, he will cast forth in ex- treme ignominy, will change their delights into torments, their laughter and joy into wailing and gnashing of teeth, their peace into the gnawing of conscience, and punish their luxury with unquenchable fire. He will also place their necks under the feet of the godly, whose patience they abused. For, as Paul declares, "it is a righteous thing with God to recompense tribu- lation to them that trouble you; and to you who are troubled rest with us, when the Lord Jesus shall be revealed from heaven." This, indeed, is our only consolation; deprived of it, we must either give way to despondency, or resort to our destruction to the vain solace of the world. The Psalmist confesses, "My feet were almost gone: my steps had well nigh slipt: for I was envious at the foolish when I saw the prosperity of the wicked"; and he found no resting-place until he entered the sanctuary, and considered the latter end of the righteous and the wicked. To conclude in one word, the

*According to Calvin, the point of all that happens in life is that we become like Jesus. That is God's ultimate mission: to do whatever is nec- essary to fashion us after his son, Jesus.*

The future life awaits us. We must keep watch. We must put our faith, peace, and hope into what is to come and not what we currently see. *That* is faith. *That* is the Christian life.

cross of Christ then only triumphs in the breasts of believers over the devil and the flesh, sin and sinners, when their eyes are directed to the power of his resurrection.

Now because the present life has always a host of delights to attract us, and has great appearance of amenity, grace, and sweetness to entice us, it is of great importance to us to be hourly withdrawn, in order that we may not be deceived, and, as it were, bewitched with such flattery.

# VITAL STATS

**WHEN AND WHERE:** St. Teresa was born in Spain in the early sixteenth century.

**STYLE:** St. Teresa was soft-hearted and mystic. Some believe her life's story is greatly exaggerated, but others hold onto her story as cold, hard truth.

**NOTEWORTHY ACCOMPLISHMENTS:** St. Teresa is known for her writings, including *Way of Perfection* and *Interior Castle*. While Martin Luther and John Calvin played influential roles in the Protestant Reformation, St. Teresa was a leader in the Counter-Reformation within the Catholic Church.

**TIMELESS WISDOM:** St. Teresa's life was marked by prayer and learning to love God and others—timeless wisdom about Christian-living basics.

You can't help but *love* the dedication of nuns. Maybe it's that all of them seem to beam from ear to ear with compassion. Or maybe it's simply because they're in the business of serving Jesus Christ. Most ordinary people just aren't that content, happy, or sincere.

Before entering the convent, most nuns have to study the lives of influential people from the past. Many of those aspiring nuns learn a great deal about St. Teresa of Ávila, one of the most famous nuns in the history of the Catholic Church. Non-Catholics might recall learning about St. Teresa while studying Christian history in church or school. It is her words here that usually move people to want to know more about this great Christian conqueror:

> *Christ has no body now on earth but yours,*
> *no hands but yours, no feet but yours;*
> *yours are the eyes through which Christ's compassion looks*
> *out on the world,*

ST. TERESA OF ÁVILA 1515–1582

*yours are the feet with which He is to go about doing good
and yours are the hands with which He is to bless us now.*[6]

These simple words are quite intriguing when you consider that St. Teresa lived a very humble and modest life. In other words, this nun lived what she preached. It doesn't take long to discover that St. Teresa was quite the ambassador for Christ in sixteenth-century Europe.

She was born in Spain in 1515. As one of ten siblings and step-siblings, Teresa lost her mother to an incurable illness at the tender age of fifteen. Her mother's death became a defining moment in this young woman's life as she had to learn quickly how to care for her younger brothers and sisters. However, not long after her mother's death, Teresa was sent to live with Augustinian nuns who cared for her until adulthood. While there, she not only studied religion, but she became a true follower of Jesus.

It was her reading of old letters by St. Jerome that inspired Teresa to enter the nun convent and dedicate herself to a full-time lifestyle of serving others. At age twenty, she entered the Carmelite Order (a well-known Spanish Catholic order). According to history, her beginning years at the convent were hardened by an accident that left both legs paralyzed for more than three years. However, she says a miraculous vision of "the sorely wounded Christ" not only healed her and allowed her to walk again, but the experience changed her spiritual life forever.

From this experience forward, Teresa became overwhelmed by the number of supernatural events in her life that inspired her to become sold out for the passion of Christ. The "miraculous" part of her life remains controversial; even today, many still pose a great deal of questions about the validity of her stories. These events, along with her great work helping the less fortunate, sealed her sainthood by the Catholic Church years after her death in 1582.

Despite the controversial aspects surrounding her life's miraculous experiences, St. Teresa's writings are inspiring works of art that deserve the attention of men and women who desire to know Jesus intimately.

She wrote from the heart—in a frank manner, really—that inspired her generation to live more boldly for Christ.

The following excerpt includes portions of chapters four and six from her book *The Way of Perfection*. St. Teresa's words about love have inspired many for years; I hope they inspire you, too.

*Matthew*

# ST. TERESA OF ÁVILA
Excerpted from *The Way of Perfection*[7]

## CHAPTER 4
### Three Habits for Effective Living

> *Exhorts the nuns to keep their Rule and names three things which are important for the spiritual life. Describes the first of these three things, which is love of one's neighbor, and speaks of the harm which can be done by individual friendships.*

Now, daughters, you have looked at the great enterprise which we are trying to carry out. What kind of persons shall we have to be if we are not to be considered over-bold in the eyes of God and of the world? It is clear that we need to labour hard and it will be a great help to us if we have sublime thoughts so that we may strive to make our actions sublime also. If we endeavor to observe our Rule and Constitutions in the fullest sense, and with great care, I hope in the Lord that He will grant our requests. I am not asking anything new of you, my daughters — only that we should hold to our profession, which, as it is our vocation, we are bound to do, although there are many ways of holding to it.

Although she believes her own audience to be primarily women, the wisdom here is not simply for females. St. Teresa's thoughts and words should be heard by men, too.

Our Primitive Rules tells us to pray without ceasing. Provided we do this with all possible care (and it is the most important thing of all) we shall not fail to observe the fasts, disciplines and periods of silence which the Order commands; for, as you know, if prayer is to be genuine it must be reinforced with these things—prayer cannot be accompanied by self-indulgence. . . .

Before speaking of the interior life—that is, of prayer—I shall speak of certain things which those who attempt to walk along the way of prayer must of necessity practise. So necessary are these that, even though not greatly given to contemplation, people who have them can advance a long way in the Lord's service, while, unless they have them, they cannot possibly be great contemplatives, and, if they think they are, they are much mistaken. May the Lord help me in this task and teach me what I must say, so that it may be to His glory. Amen.

*Interesting. How often do we pray without thinking about whether our daily habits, actions, and attitudes are pleasing to God?*

Do not suppose, my friends and sisters, that I am going to charge you to do a great many things; may it please the Lord that we do the things which our holy Fathers ordained and practised and by doing which they merited that name. It would be wrong of us to look for any other way or to learn from anyone else. There are only three things which I will explain at some length and which are taken from our [Church] Constitution itself. It is essential that we should understand how very important they are to us in helping us to preserve that peace, both inward and outward, which the Lord so earnestly recommended to us. One of these is love for each other; the second, detachment from all created things; the third, true humility, which, although I put it last, is the most important of the three and embraces all the rest.

*Remember, St. Teresa was a nun; it was her desire to stay away from all worldliness. She knew how easily we're distracted by worldliness and materialism, which can take over our priorities if we're not careful to stay focused on God. Now for more about love . . .*

### Can't Get Enough about Love

With regard to the first—namely, love for each other—this is of very great importance; for there is nothing, however annoying, that cannot easily be borne by those who love each other, and anything which causes annoyance must be quite exceptional. If this commandment were kept in the world, as it should be, I believe it would take us a long way towards the keeping of the rest; but, what with having too much love for each other or too little, we never manage to keep it perfectly. It may seem that for us to have too much love for each other cannot be wrong, but I do not think anyone who had not been an eye-witness of it would believe how much evil and how many imperfections can result from this. The devil sets many snares here which the consciences of those who aim only in a rough-and-ready way at pleasing God seldom observe—indeed, they think they are acting virtuously—but those who are aiming at perfection understand what they are very well: little by little they deprive the will of the strength which it needs if it is to employ itself wholly in the love of God. . . .

Returning to the question of our love for one another, it seems quite unnecessary to commend this to you, for where are there people so brutish as not to love one another when they live together, are continually in one another's company, indulge in no conversation, association or recreation with any outside their house and believe that God loves us and that they themselves love God since they are leaving everything for His Majesty? More especially is this so as virtue always attracts love, and I hope in God that, with the help of His Majesty, there will always be love in the sisters of this house. It seems to me, therefore, that there is no reason for me to commend this to you any further. . . .

St. Teresa believed that loving others is one of the most basic Christian practices. It's at the core of what it means to be a lover of Jesus.

There are two kinds of love which I am describing. The one is *purely* spiritual, and apparently has nothing to do with sensuality or the tenderness of our nature, either of which might stain its purity. The other is also spiritual, but mingled with it are our sensuality and weakness; yet it is a worthy love, which, as between relatives and friends, seems lawful. Of this I have already said sufficient.

It is of the first kind of spiritual love that I

would now speak. It is untainted by any sort of passion, for such a thing would completely spoil its harmony. . . .

## CHAPTER 6
### God's Perfect Love Perfects Our Love for Others
**Returns to the subject of perfect love, already begun.**

Let us now return to the love which it is good [and lawful] for us to feel. This I have described as purely spiritual; I am not sure if I know what I am talking about, but it seems to me that there is no need to speak much of it, since so few, I fear, possess it; let any one of you to whom the Lord has given it praise Him fervently, for she must be a person of the greatest perfection. It is about this that I now wish to write. Perhaps what I say may be of some profit, for if you look at a virtue you desire it and try to gain it, and so become attached to it. . . .

Now it seems to me that, when God has brought someone to a clear knowledge of the world, and of its nature, and of the fact that another world (*or, let us say, another kingdom*) exists, and that there is a great difference between the one and the other, the one being eternal and the other only a dream; and of what it is to love the Creator and what to love the creature (this must

> Her thoughts on spiritual love are quite interesting when you consider that much of the love we offer is a form of tenderness or sensuality.

be discovered by experience, for it is a very different matter from merely thinking about it and believing it); when one understands by sight and experience what can be gained by the one practice and lost by the other, and what the Creator is and what the creature, and many other things which the Lord teaches to those who are willing to devote themselves to being taught by Him in prayer, or whom His Majesty wishes to teach—then one loves very differently from those of us who have not advanced thus far.

It may be, sisters, that you think it irrelevant for me to treat of this, and you may say that you already know everything that I have said. God grant that this may be so, and that you may indeed know it in the only way which has any meaning, and that it may be graven upon your inmost being, *and that you may never for a moment depart from it*, for, if you know it, you will see that I am telling nothing but the truth when I say that he whom the Lord brings thus far possesses this love. Those whom God brings to this state are, *I think*, generous and royal souls; they are not content with loving anything so miserable as these bodies, however beautiful they be and however numerous the graces they possess. If the sight of the body gives them pleasure they praise the Creator, but as for dwelling upon it *for more than just a moment*—no! When I use that phrase "dwelling upon it," I refer to having love for such things. If they had such love, they would think they were loving something insubstantial and were conceiving fondness for a shadow, they would feel shame for themselves and would not have the effrontery to tell God that they love Him, without feeling great confusion.

Basically, St. Teresa is saying that, once a person experiences the deep, lasting, and perfect love of God, all other affections pale in comparison. However, she'll soon make the powerful point that, once we have God's perfect love ingrained in us, it causes us to want to extend that love to others—particularly to those who've also experienced God-size love.

You will answer me that such persons cannot love or repay the affection shown to them by others. Certainly they care little about having this affection. They may from time to time experience a natural and momentary pleasure at being loved; yet, as soon as they return to their normal condition, they realize that such pleasure is folly save when the persons concerned can benefit their souls, either by instruction or by prayer. Any other kind of affection wearies them, for they know it can bring them no profit and may well do them harm; none the less they are grateful for it and recompense it by commending those who love them to God. . . .

It should be noted here that, when we desire anyone's affection, we always seek it because of some interest, profit or pleasure of our own. Those who are perfect, however, have trodden all these things beneath their feet—[and have de-

spised] the blessings which may come to them in this world, and its pleasures and delights—in such a way that, even if they wanted to, so to say,
they could not love anything outside God, or unless it had to do with God.
What profit, then, can come to them from being loved themselves?

## Love Keeps Giving

When this truth is put to them, they laugh at the distress which had been
assailing them in the past as to whether their affection was being returned
or no. Of course, however pure our affection may be, it is quite natural for
us to wish it to be returned. But, when we come to evaluate the return of affection, we realize that it is insubstantial, like a thing of straw, as light as air
and easily carried away by the wind. For, however dearly we have been
loved, what is there that remains to us? Such persons, then, except for the
advantage that the affection may bring to their souls (because they realize
that our nature is such that we soon tire of life without love), care nothing
whether they are loved or not. Do you think that such persons will love
none and delight in none save God? No; they will love others much more
than they did, with a more genuine love, with greater passion and with a
love which brings more profit; that, in a word, is what love really is. And
such souls are always much fonder of giving than of receiving, even in their
relations with the Creator Himself. This [holy affection], I say, merits the
name of love, which name has been usurped from it by those other base
affections.

## Love Looks Deep—and Lasts Forever

Do you ask, again, by what they are attracted if they do not love things they
see? They do love what they see and they are greatly attracted by what they
hear; but the things which they see are everlasting. If they love anyone they
immediately look right beyond the body *(on which, as I say, they cannot
dwell)*, fix their eyes on the soul and see what there is to be loved in that. If
there is nothing, but they see any suggestion or inclination which shows
them that, if they dig deep, they will find gold within this mine, they think

nothing of the labour of digging, since they have love. There is nothing that suggests itself to them which they will not willingly do for the good of that soul since they desire their love for it to be lasting, and they know quite well that that is impossible unless the loved one has certain good qualities and a great love for God. I really mean that it is impossible, however great their obligations and even if that soul were to die for love of them and do them all the kind actions in its power; even had it all the natural graces joined in one, their wills would not have strength enough to love it nor would they remain fixed upon it. They know and have learned and experienced the worth of all this; no false dice can deceive them. They see that they are not in unison with that soul and that their love for it cannot possibly last; for, unless that soul keeps the law of God, their love will end with life—they know that unless it loves Him they will go to different places.

> If one person loves God but the other doesn't, their whole perspective of love isn't united at its core. On the other hand, two people who share God's perfect love can enjoy a love of the eternal kind!

Those into whose souls the Lord has already infused true wisdom do not esteem this love, which lasts only on earth, at more than its true worth—if, indeed, at so much. Those who like to take pleasure in worldly things, delights, honours and riches, will account it of some worth if their friend is rich and able to afford them pastime *and pleasure* and recreation; but those who already hate all this will care little or nothing for such things. If they have any love for such a person, then, it will be a passion that he may love God so as to be loved by Him; for, as I say, they know that no other kind of affection but this can last, and that this kind will cost them dear, for which reason they do all they possibly can for their friend's profit; they would lose a thousand lives to bring him a small blessing. Oh, precious love, forever imitating the Captain of Love, Jesus, our Good!

# VITAL STATS

**WHEN AND WHERE:** Born Nicolas Herman of Lorraine, he was a soldier for France most of his young adult years. At age fifty-five, he joined the Carmelite Order (the same order as St. Teresa of Ávila) as a lay brother where he spent most of his remaining years as a cook. Outside the monastery, France was an ambitious country and hungry for more power, prestige, and control.

**STYLE:** Brother Lawrence came from a very meager background and was not a learned man. He lived a quiet, reflective life in the kitchen at his monastery. He was known for his authentic, simple faith and for his selfless service to others.

**NOTEWORTHY ACCOMPLISHMENTS:** His practical faith had a positive impact throughout France even before his death. After his passing, two volumes of writings and conversations were published, and they have inspired readers all over the world ever since.

**TIMELESS WISDOM:** True faith is a relationship. It is a constant state of communion between a person and God at all times, as natural as breathing . . . as beautiful as life itself. Enjoying the presence of God can be as simple as lifting your eyes up to him in every instant, not *instead of* doing other things, but *in the midst of* daily life.

You've been reading some pretty heavy stuff in this book. Deep, profound, life-changing theology, written by remarkable men and women with uncommon spiritual insight, that has truly altered the course of history. Knowing the impact these great authors of the past have made through the years is cool to think about, but dude . . . it can be overwhelming! Were they on spiritual steroids or something? Did they ever sleep or take midterms? When did they find time to wash clothes and go to the grocery store?

They were undoubtedly amazing multitaskers back then. They had to be, or they couldn't possibly have thought,

**BROTHER LAWRENCE** c. 1605–1691

prayed, and written so much. You know, it's not a documented or proven fact or anything, but Brother Lawrence might well have been one of the greatest multitaskers of all time. And yet, surprisingly he was the exact opposite of ADD. Instead of Attention *Deficit* Disorder, he seemed to have Attention *Surplus* that always led him to order and peace and rest.

This rather ordinary French man lived a rather boring life. He grew up very poor and was not formally educated. Brother Lawrence was a soldier for most of his early adulthood. He wasn't exactly what you would call a deep theological thinker, either. But he had a relationship with Christ that was so pure, so real and authentic, that it still inspires people four hundred years later!

Nicolas wanted to have more time to spend pondering, worshipping, and conversing with God, so he left his life of public service behind, changed his name, and became a monk in the religious community of the Carmelites. At the monastery, Brother Lawrence volunteered for the lowest and most trivial tasks. He spent hours in the kitchen every day preparing and serving food to the other monks.

He felt that he had no special gifts to offer the Lord, but he loved him so much that he made it his life's goal to learn how to remain in the presence of God at all times. Every time his mind would wander off Christ, he would take the stray thought captive and place it right back on the Lord. Can't you just see him there in the kitchen, peeling potatoes and baking cornbread, all the while contemplating the wonder and majesty of the One who created the crops and the sun and the rain? Apparently the constant conversation he enjoyed with God was obvious even from his outward appearance, because the other friars and monks took notice. He became an inspiration to them in their own walks of faith.

The following excerpts are from some of his letters. He talks about how to literally converse with the Father at all times. When we focus our attention on him, the result is a constant companionship that gives meaning to life and causes all the things of earth to "grow strangely dim."

Brother Lawrence's work is not a deep, heavily theological masterpiece. You won't need to read the sentences more than once to get their meaning. In fact, you may even find his wisdom simplistic in nature. But give his methods a try and see how "simple" it seems as you peel your dinner potatoes next time. You'll quickly understand why it's called the *practice* of the presence of God! It definitely takes discipline and practice. Don't be discouraged, though, and don't allow yourself to be too quick to condemn yourself when your mind strays. Brother Lawrence struggled when he first started too.

Even so, he kept refocusing his attention until in his later years constant communion with Christ came as naturally as breathing for him. As a result, his life overflowed with joy, love, and selfless service to God and others. Whatever task he undertook always shared mind space with the constant contemplation of his God. Now *that's* multitasking we all need to learn!

*Janella*

# BROTHER LAWRENCE
Excerpted from *The Practice of the Presence of God*[8]

## FIRST LETTER
### It's All about God

This made me resolve to give the all for the All: so after having given myself wholly to GOD, to make all the satisfaction I could for my sins, I renounced, for the love of Him, everything that was not He; and I began to live as if there was none but He and I in the world.

Sometimes I considered myself before Him as a poor criminal at the feet of his judge; at other times I beheld Him in my heart as my FATHER, as my GOD: I worshipped Him the oftenest that I could, keeping my mind in His holy Presence, and recalling it as often as I found it wandered from Him. I found no small pain in this exercise, and yet I continued it, notwithstanding all the difficulties that occurred, without troubling or disquieting myself when my mind had wandered involuntarily. I made this my business, as much all the day long as at the appointed times of prayer; for at all times, every hour, every minute, even in the height of my business, I drove away from my mind everything that was capable of interrupting my thought of GOD.

Does your mind ever wander when you're trying to spend time with God? Even Brother Lawrence had that problem. But he just kept *practicing*. No berating himself. No giving up because it was too hard. No whining. Just a passionate determination to live in the presence of God.

## SECOND LETTER
### Breaking Through to God's Presence

Such was my beginning; and yet I must tell you, that for the first ten years I suffered much: the apprehension that I was not devoted to GOD, as I wished to be, my past sins always present to my mind, and the great unmerited favours which GOD did me, were the matter and source of my sufferings. During this time I fell often, and rose again presently. It seemed to me that the creatures, reason, and GOD Himself were against me; And faith alone for me.

When I thought of nothing but to end my days in these troubles (which did not at all diminish the trust I had in GOD, and which served only to increase my faith), I found myself changed all at once; and my soul, which till that time was in trouble, felt a profound inward peace, as if she were in her centre and place of rest. Ever since that time I walk before GOD simply, in faith, with humility and with love; and I apply myself diligently to do nothing and think nothing which may displease Him. I hope that when I have done what I can, He will do with me what He pleases.

> Brother Lawrence got to the point of true and constant communion with God, as natural as the ebbing tides. All that time spent in the presence purified his motives . . . and it seems like motives are pretty important to God.

As for what passes in me at present, I cannot express it. I have no pain or difficulty about my state, because I have no will but that of GOD, which I endeavour to accomplish in all things, and to which I am so resigned, that I would not take up a straw from the ground against His order, or from any other motive but purely that of love to Him.

## FOURTH LETTER

### Visible Signs of God's Presence

You must know, his continual care has been, for above forty years past that he has spent in religion, to be always with GOD; and to do nothing,

> Notice he writes of himself in the third person in this letter.

say nothing, and think nothing which may displease Him; and this without any other view than purely for the love of Him, and because He deserves infinitely more.

He is now so accustomed to that Divine presence, that he receives from it continual succours upon all occasions. For about thirty years, his soul has been filled with joys so continual, and sometimes so great, that he is forced to use means to moderate them, and to hinder their appearing outwardly.

## FIFTH LETTER

### *A Heart Open for God's Business*

What a shame that he had to "moderate" the outward expression of inward joy! Wouldn't you love to see this old monk jumping up and down, shouting, "Hallelujah!" in the kitchen while all the other monks were in line for their supper?

I will send you one of those books which treat of the presence of GOD; a subject which, in my opinion, contains the whole spiritual life; and it seems to me that whoever duly practises it will soon become spiritual.

I know that for the right practice of it, the heart must be empty of all other things; because GOD will possess the heart alone; and as He cannot possess it alone, without emptying it of all besides, so neither can He act there, and do in it what He pleases, unless it be left vacant to Him.

There is not in the world a kind of life more sweet and delightful, than that of a continual conversation with GOD: those only can comprehend it who practise and experience it; yet I do not advise you to do it from that motive; it is not pleasure which we ought to seek in this exercise; but let us do it from a principle of love, and because GOD would have us.

Brother Lawrence makes an excellent point here—religious persons do not automatically live in the practice of the presence of God. That comes from a love relationship, not from a religion!

## SIXTH LETTER

### *Unimaginable Life without God*

I cannot imagine how religious persons can live satisfied without the practice of the presence of GOD. For my part I keep myself retired with Him in the depth of centre of my soul as much as I can; and while I am so with Him I fear nothing; but the least turning from Him is insupportable.

## SEVENTH LETTER
### Being with God in the Everyday

I PITY you much. It will be of great importance if you can leave the care of your affairs to, and spend the remainder of your life only in worshipping GOD. He requires no great matters of us; a little remembrance of Him from time to time, a little adoration: sometimes to pray for His grace, sometimes to offer Him your sufferings, and sometimes to return Him thanks for the favours He has given you, and still gives you, in the midst of your troubles, and to console yourself with Him the oftenest you can. Lift up your heart to Him, sometimes even at your meals, and when you are in company: the least little remembrance will always be acceptable to Him. You need not cry very loud; He is nearer to us than we are aware of.

It is not necessary for being with GOD to be always at church; we may make an oratory of our heart, wherein to retire from time to time, to converse with Him in meekness, humility, and love. Every one is capable of such familiar conversation with GOD, some more, some less: He knows what we can do. Let us begin then; perhaps He expects but one generous resolution on our part. Have courage. We have but little time to live.

## EIGHTH LETTER
### Battling Wandering Thoughts

YOU tell me nothing new: you are not the only one that is troubled with wandering thoughts. Our mind is extremely roving; but as the will is mistress of all our faculties, she must recall them, and carry them to GOD, as their last end.

When the mind, for want of being sufficiently reduced by recollection, at our first engaging in devotion, has contracted certain bad habits of wandering and dissipation, they are difficult to overcome, and commonly draw us, even against our wills, to the things of the earth.

I believe one remedy for this is, to confess our faults, and to humble ourselves before GOD. I do not advise you to use multiplicity of words in prayer; many words and long discourses being often the occasions of wandering: hold yourself in prayer before GOD, like a dumb or paralytic beggar at a rich man's gate: let it be your business to keep your mind in the presence of the LORD. If it sometimes wander, and withdraw itself from Him, do not much disquiet yourself for that; trouble and disquiet serve rather to distract the mind, than to re-collect it; the will must bring it back in tranquillity; if you persevere in this manner, GOD will have pity on you.

> What a relief that we don't have to figure out the "right" words when we pray. Prayer is simply sharing our thoughts and feelings.

One way to re-collect the mind easily in the time of prayer, and preserve it more in tranquillity, is not to let it wander too far at other times: you should keep it strictly in the presence of GOD; and being accustomed to think of Him often, you will find it easy to keep your mind calm in the time of prayer, or at least to recall it from its wanderings.

## NINTH LETTER

### Developing the Habit

THE enclosed is an answer to that which I received from - ; pray deliver it to her. She seems to me full of good will, but she would go faster than grace. One does not become holy all at once. . . .

We cannot escape the dangers which abound in life, without the actual and continual help of GOD; let us then pray to Him for it continually. How can we pray to Him without being with Him? How can we be with Him but in thinking of Him often? And how can we often think of Him, but by a holy habit which we should form of it? You will tell me that I am always saying the same thing: it is true, for this is the best and easiest method I know; and as I use no other, I advise all the world to it. We must know before we can love. In order to know GOD, we must often think of Him; and when we come to love Him, we shall then also think of Him often, for our heart will be with our treasure. This is an argument which well deserves your consideration.

## TWELFTH LETTER
### Hang in There with God
Take courage, offer Him your pains incessantly, pray to Him for strength to endure them. Above all, get a habit of entertaining yourself often with GOD, and forget Him the least you can. Adore Him in your infirmities, offer yourself to Him from time to time; and, in the height of your sufferings, beseech Him humbly and affectionately (as a child his father) to make you conformable to His holy will. I shall endeavour to assist you with my poor prayers.

GOD has many ways of drawing us to Himself. He sometimes hides Himself from us: but faith alone, which will not fail us in time of need, ought to be our support, and the foundation of our confidence, which must be all in GOD. . . .

I would willingly ask of GOD a part of your sufferings, but that I know my weakness, which is so great, that if He left me one moment to myself, I should be the most wretched man alive. And yet I know not how He can leave me alone, because faith gives me as strong a conviction as sense can do, that He never forsakes us, till we have first forsaken Him. Let us fear to leave Him. Let us be always with Him. Let us live and die in His presence. Do you pray for me, as I for you.

## FIFTEENTH LETTER
### Knowing God Defines Our Perspective
GOD knoweth best what is needful for us, and all that He does is for our good. If we knew how much He loves us, we should be always ready to receive equally and with indifference from His hand the sweet and the bitter; all would please that came from Him. The sorest afflictions never appear intolerable, but when we see them in the wrong light. When we see them in the hand of GOD, who dispenses them: when we know that it is our loving FATHER, who abases and distresses us: our sufferings will lose their bitterness, and become even matter of consolation.

Let all our employment be to know GOD: the more one knows Him,

Many people all over the world know *about* God, but the goal is to really *know God* on a deep, intimate, personal heart level.

the more one desires to know Him. And as knowledge is commonly the measure of love, the deeper and more extensive our knowledge shall be, the greater will be our love: and if our love of GOD were great we should love Him equally in pains and pleasures.

Let us not amuse ourselves to seek or to love GOD for any sensible favours (how elevated soever) which He has or may do us. Such favours, though never so great, cannot bring us so near to GOD as faith does in one simple act. Let us seek Him often by faith: He is within us; seek Him not elsewhere. Are we not rude and deserve blame, if we leave Him alone, to busy ourselves about trifles, which do not please Him and perhaps offend Him? 'Tis to be feared these trifles will one day cost us dear.

The idea of the "prosperity gospel" you see late at night on religious television, "name-it-and-claim-it" faith, is not biblical and is certainly not a pure motive for seeking to love God!

Let us begin to be devoted to Him in good earnest. Let us cast everything besides out of our hearts; He would possess them alone. Beg this favour of Him. If we do what we can on our parts, we shall soon see that change wrought in us which we aspire after. I cannot thank Him sufficiently for the relaxation He has vouchsafed you. I hope from His mercy the favour to see Him within a few days. Let us pray for one another.

# VITAL STATS

**WHEN AND WHERE:** John Bunyan's writing and preaching impacted England during the seventeenth century. He began preaching in 1655 after his wife led him to Christ.

**STYLE:** Bunyan's preaching style was hard-nosed and scandalous—especially to the rich. Refusal to change the fiery presentation of his words put him in jail for twelve years.

**NOTEWORTHY ACCOMPLISHMENT:** *The Pilgrim's Progress* is one of the best-selling books of all time. For a while, only the King James Version of the Bible had sold more worldwide.

**TIMELESS WISDOM:** John Bunyan was constantly searching for holiness. He longed to see it in his own life and longed to help others pursue it.

I was in eighth grade when I first learned of *The Pilgrim's Progress* by John Bunyan. Considering Bunyan had been dead for several hundred years, I was not too enthralled when my teacher announced that our class would be expected to read the narrative and write a two-page summary about what we learned from the literary experience. Just from staring at the book's cover picture of John with his long seventeenth-century locks, I was thoroughly convinced that the only things I could possibly learn from this dead man's book were going to be boring, religious, and irrelevant to my life.

You know what? I was right! The first time I read *The Pilgrim's Progress* I did think all those things. But give me a break; I was in eighth grade. Even though I had been following Jesus since I was four years old, I didn't have the spiritual depth then to appreciate Bunyan's historical work.

However, in early 2004, I was fumbling through some old books of my mom's and found that old copy of the book. At first, it brought back horrendous memories about being an awkward ad-olescent trying not to fall asleep as I attempted to work my way through Christian's long journey toward heaven. But as those memories swirled through my head, I decided my first trek through this book had been jaded by immaturity and that I should give it another chance. So I did.

This time, the book came alive for me. Many years had gone by and a lot of life was lived since eighth grade. As I reread Bunyan's story of God's hold on Christian, I noticed many similarities to my own story. I also had a new appreciation for the basic truth this book communi-cated. After I completed the tale, I reacquainted myself with Bunyan's biography.

John Bunyan was a theological scholar and a pastor who grew up in England during the mid-1600s. His first wife led him to Christ when he was around twenty years old. Five years later, he left his work as a ma-chine tinker and became a preacher. He eventually became well-known to the world around him as a Bible-thumping troublemaker. Conse-quently, he was thrown into prison for refusing to alter the topics and fi-ery nature of his sermons. At one point in his career, he was imprisoned for twelve years. It was during this sentence that he wrote the narrative that would become *The Pilgrim's Progress.*

In 1678, his first volume of the work was published and eventually be-came an international best seller. In fact, for more than three hundred years, the King James Version of the Bible was the only book to outsell *The Pilgrim's Progress.*

Perhaps you're like me—you read the book years ago but hardly gave it a chance. Or maybe you're hearing about it for the first time right now. Below you'll find an excerpt from this great, influential book. It's a conversation between Christian, the story's protagonist, and Hopeful, one of many people Christian meets on his long journey. While you're reading, be sure to notice Bunyan's wide use of Scripture. In his writing, he desired to make sure that the Word of God was represented purely and literally.

After completing this excerpt, I recommend you buy the whole book and read the simple tale from start to finish. Then, write a two-page report on what you learned. . . . *I'm kidding.* Just enjoy the journey and revel in the spiritual secrets about a Christian's life John Bunyan recognized many years ago.

*Matthew*

## JOHN BUNYAN

Excerpted from *The Pilgrim's Progress*[9]

Yes, this book is written in old English. It might take you a moment to get used to the *thines* and *thees*, but fret not! Just pretend you're a well-known Shakespearian actor reading your part of the script.

### Stuck in the Trap of Sin

CHRISTIAN: How came you to think at first of doing what you do now?

HOPEFUL: Do you mean, How came I at first to look after the good of my soul?

CHRISTIAN: Yes, that is my meaning.

HOPEFUL: I continued a great while in the delight of those things which were seen and sold at our fair; things which, I believe now, would have (had I continued in them still) drowned me in perdition and destruction.

CHRISTIAN: What things were they?

HOPEFUL: All the treasures and riches of the world. Also I delighted much in rioting, revelling, drinking, swearing, lying, uncleanness, Sabbath-breaking, and what not, that tended to destroy the soul. But I found at last, by hearing and considering of things that are divine, which, indeed I heard of you, as also of beloved Faithful, that was put to death for his faith and good living in Vanity Fair, that 'the end of these things is death.' And that for these things' sake the wrath of God cometh upon the children of disobedience.

Hopeful's list of sins would look pretty much the same if this book had been written today. Perhaps its timelessness is what has kept readers turning the story's pages for all these generations.

CHRISTIAN: And did you presently fall under the power of this conviction?

HOPEFUL: No, I was not willing presently to know the evil of sin, nor the damnation that follows upon the commission of it; but endeavored, when my mind at first began to be shaken with the Word, to shut mine eyes against the light thereof.

CHRISTIAN: But what was the cause of your carrying of it thus to the first workings of God's blessed Spirit upon you?

HOPEFUL: The causes were: 1. I was ignorant that this was the work of God upon me. I never thought that by awakenings for sin God at first begins the conversion of a sinner. 2. Sin was yet very sweet to my flesh, and I was loth to leave it. 3. I could not tell how to part with my old companions, their presence and actions were so desirable unto me. 4. The hours in which convictions were upon me, were such troublesome and such heart-affrighting hours, that I could not bear, no not so much as the remembrance of them upon my heart.

CHRISTIAN: Then as it seems, sometimes you got rid of your trouble?

HOPEFUL: Yes, verily; but it would come into my mind again, and then I would be as bad, nay worse, than I was before.

CHRISTIAN: Why, what was it that brought your sins to mind again?

> All of us have moments in our lives when sin seems very sweet and we're "loath to leave it," when we can't (or won't) see truth because our hearts and minds and bodies are indulging in what the world deems necessary. Bunyan is never afraid to reveal the ugly side of human nature.

HOPEFUL: Many things: as:

1. If I did but meet a good man in the streets; or,

2. If I have heard any read in the Bible; or,

3. If mine head did begin to ache; or,

4. If I were told that some of my neighbors were sick; or,

5. If I heard the bell toll for some that were dead; or,

6. If I thought of dying myself; or,

7. If I heard that sudden death happened to others;

8. But especially, when I thought of myself, that I must quickly come to judgment.

Hopeful's biggest problem may not have been the actual sin, but the guilt that haunted him afterwards.

CHRISTIAN: And could you at any time, with ease, get off the guilt of sin, when by any of these ways it came upon you?

HOPEFUL: No, not latterly, for then they got faster hold of my conscience; and then, if I did but think of going back to sin (though my mind was turned against it), it would be double torment to me.

## Fixing the Problem?

CHRISTIAN: And how did you do then?

HOPEFUL: I thought I must endeavor to mend my life; for else, thought I, I am sure to be damned.

CHRISTIAN: And did you endeavor to mend?

HOPEFUL: Yes, and fled from, not only my sins, but sinful company too; and betook me to religious duties, as praying, reading, weeping for sin, speaking truth to my neighbours, etc. These things did I, with many others, too much here to relate.

Guilt often makes us try to earn God's acceptance by saying and doing all the "right" things. But as you will see, Hopeful's performance did not last. It worked for a while, but ended up being futile.

CHRISTIAN: And did you think yourself well then?

HOPEFUL: Yes, for a while; but at the last my trouble came tumbling upon me again, and that over the neck of all my reformation.

CHRISTIAN: How came that about, since you were now reformed?

HOPEFUL: There were several things brought it upon me, especially such sayings as these: 'All our righteousness are as filthy rags.' 'By the works of the law no man shall be justified.'

'When you have done all these things, say, We are unprofitable,': with many more such like. From whence I began to reason with myself thus: If all my righteousness are filthy rags, if by the deeds of the law, no man can be justified; and if, when we have done all, we are yet unprofitable, then 'tis but a folly to think of heaven by the law. I further thought thus: If a man runs a hundred pounds into the shopkeeper's debt, and after that shall pay for all that he shall fetch; yet if his old debt stand still in the book uncrossed, for that the shopkeeper may sue him, and cast him into prison, till he shall pay the debt.

CHRISTIAN: Well, and how did you apply this to yourself?

HOPEFUL: Why, I thought thus with myself: I have by my sins run a great way into God's Book, and that my now reforming will not pay off that score; therefore I would think still under all my present amendments, But how shall I be freed from that damnation that I brought myself in danger of by my former transgressions?

"We are all infected and impure with sin. When we display our righteous deeds, they are nothing but filthy rags" (Isaiah 64:6). All the good we do isn't enough to save us. So now what?

CHRISTIAN: A very good application: but pray go on.

HOPEFUL: Another thing that hath troubled me, even since my late amendments, is, that if I look narrowly into the best of what I do now, I still see sin, new sin, mixing itself with the best of that I do; so that now I am forced to conclude, that notwithstanding my former fond conceits of myself and duties, I have committed sin enough in one day to send me to hell, though my former life had been faultless.

CHRISTIAN: And what did you do then?

HOPEFUL: Do! I could not tell what to do, till I brake my mind to Faithful, for he and I were well acquainted. And he told me, that unless I could obtain the righteousness of a man that never had sinned, neither mine own, nor all the righteousness of the world could save me.

Hopeful's friend Faithful proved to him with Scripture that even his good deeds were flawed and incapable of saving him.

CHRISTIAN: And did you think he spake true?

HOPEFUL: Had he told me so when I was pleased and satisfied with my own amendments, I had called him fool for his pains; but now, since I see my own infirmity, and the sin that cleaves to my best performance, I have been forced to be of his opinion.

CHRISTIAN: But did you think, when at first he suggested it to you, that there was such a man to be found, of whom it might justly be said, That he never committed sin?

### The Solution at Last

HOPEFUL: I must confess the words at first sounded strangely; but after a little more talk and company with him, I had full conviction about it.

CHRISTIAN: And did you ask him what man this was, and how you must be justified by him?

HOPEFUL: Yes, and he told me it was the Lord Jesus, that dwelleth on the right hand of the Most High. And thus, said he, you must be justified by him, even by trusting to what he hath done by himself in the days of his flesh, and suffered when he did hang on the tree. I asked him further, How that man's righteousness could be of that efficacy, to justify another before God? And he told me, He was the "mighty God," and did what he did, and died the death also, not for himself, but for me; to whom his doings, and the worthiness of them, should be imputed, if I believed on him.

CHRISTIAN: And what did you do then?

HOPEFUL: I made my objections against my believing, for that I thought he was not willing to save me.

CHRISTIAN: And what said Faithful to you then?

HOPEFUL: He bid me go to Him and see. Then I said it was presumption: He said, No; for I was invited to come. Then he gave me a book of Jesus his inditing, to encourage me the more freely to come; and he said concerning that book, that every jot and tittle thereof stood firmer than heaven and earth. Then I asked him, What I must do when I came? and he told me, I must entreat upon my knees, with all my heart and soul, the Father to reveal him to me. Then I asked him further, How I must make my supplication to him? and he said, Go, and thou shalt find him upon a mercy-seat, where he sits all the year long to give pardon and forgiveness to them that come. I told him that I knew not what to say when I came. And he bid me say to this ef-

*Bunyan is famous for lacing his stories with Scripture. I like that about him.*

fect: God be merciful to me a sinner, and make me to know and believe in Jesus Christ; for I see that if his righteousness had not been, or I have not faith in that righteousness, I am utterly cast away. . . .

CHRISTIAN: And did you do as you were bidden?

HOPEFUL: Yes; over, and over, and over.

CHRISTIAN: And did the Father reveal his Son to you?

HOPEFUL: Not at the first, nor second, nor third, nor fourth, nor fifth, no, nor at the sixth time neither.

CHRISTIAN: What did you do then?

HOPEFUL: What! why, I could not tell what to do.

CHRISTIAN: Had you not thoughts of leaving off praying?

HOPEFUL: Yes; and a hundred times, twice told.

CHRISTIAN: And what was the reason you did not?

HOPEFUL: I believed that that was true which hath been told me, to wit, That without the righteousness of this Christ, all the world could not save me; and therefore thought I with myself, If I leave off, I die; and I can but die at the throne of grace. And withal, this came into my mind: 'If it tarry, wait for it; because it will surely come, and will not tarry.' So I continued praying until the Father showed me his Son.

CHRISTIAN: And how was he revealed unto you?

HOPEFUL: I did *not* see him with my bodily eyes, but with the eyes of mine understanding; and thus it was: One day I was very sad, I think sadder than at any one time in my life, and this sadness was through a fresh sight of the greatness and vileness of my sins. And as I was then looking for nothing but hell, and the everlasting damnation of my soul, suddenly, as I thought, I saw the Lord Jesus look down from heaven upon me, and saying, 'Believe on the Lord Jesus Christ, and thou shalt be saved.'

But I replied, Lord, I am a great, a very great sinner: and he answered, 'My grace is sufficient for thee.' Then I said, But, Lord, what is believing? And then I saw from that saying, ['He that cometh to me shall never hunger, and he that believeth on me shall never thirst'], that believing and coming was all one; and that he that came, that is, that ran out in his heart and affections after salvation by Christ, he indeed believed in Christ. Then the water stood in mine eyes, and I asked further, But, Lord, may such a great sinner as I am be indeed accepted of thee, and be saved by thee? And I heard him say, 'And him that cometh to me I will in no wise cast out.' Then I said, But how, Lord, must I consider of thee in my coming to thee, that my faith may be placed aright upon thee? Then he said, 'Christ Jesus came into the world to save sinners.' 'He is the end of the law for righteousness to every one that believes.' 'He died for our sins, and rose again for our justification: He loved us, and washed us from our sins in his own blood.' 'He is Mediator between God and us.' 'He ever liveth to make intercession for us.' From all which I gathered, that I must look for righteousness in his person, and for satisfaction for my sins by his blood; that what he did in obedience to his Father's law, and in submitting to the penalty thereof, was not for himself, but for him that will accept it for his salvation, and be thankful. And now was my heart full of joy, mine eyes full of tears, and mine affections running over with love to the name, people, and ways of Jesus Christ.

At last, after relentless searching, Hopeful finally understood that Jesus Christ died to save him *and* to help him live right.

CHRISTIAN: This was a revelation of Christ to your soul indeed; but tell me particularly what effect this had upon your spirit.

HOPEFUL: It made me see that all the world, notwithstanding all the righteousness thereof, is in a state of condemnation. It made me see that God the Father, though he be just, can justly justify the coming sinner. It made me greatly ashamed of the vileness of my former life, and confounded me with the sense of mine own ignorance; for there never came a thought into my heart before now, that showed me so the beauty of Jesus Christ. It made me love a holy life, and long to do something for the honor and glory of the name of the Lord Jesus. Yea, I thought that had I now a thousand gallons of blood in my body, I could spill it all for the sake of the Lord Jesus.

Hopeful finally found the joy and peace that comes from a relationship with Jesus. Bunyan's story of Christian's journey became one of the most famous salvation stories ever told.

# VITAL STATS

**WHEN AND WHERE:** In an age when society kept women silent and subservient, Madame Guyon was instrumental in showing many that it was possible to have a dynamic spiritual relationship with God.

**STYLE:** Her passion was prayer. When her own family fought her to keep her from praying, she would rise in the middle of the night to spend time in prayer while everyone else slept. With quiet resolve she expressed her controversial beliefs about Quietism and knowing God on a deeply personal level.

**NOTEWORTHY ACCOMPLISHMENTS:** Madame Guyon became very influential in the French courts, where she helped many women live such lives of purity that they easily stood out against the lavish and sexually immoral lives of those around them. She maintained her stance on purity and prayer and spent several years in prison for her steadfast teaching about experiencing God.

**TIMELESS WISDOM:** "Prayer is the guide to perfection, and prayer delivers us from every vice, and gives us every virtue; for the one way to become perfect is to walk in the presence of God." Madame Guyon's example inspires us to wonder what miracles God may do in our time if we dedicate ourselves to growing in personal prayer.

The unforgiving walls of the prison cell hung like a shroud, letting in enough dim light to reveal rats loitering in the corners. Occasionally one would dare approach her huddled form, sometimes willing to be shooed away, other times hanging nearby, taunting. The thought of a disease-ridden rodent bite was eclipsed only by the horrible stench of her own waste. She flexed her fingers again, willing a meager measure of body heat to trickle past each knuckle so she could write one more sentence. . . .

Few people in the history of the world have lived and breathed their dedication to God as powerfully as Madame

**MADAME GUYON 1648–1717**

Jeanne Guyon. This woman's gentle strength and faith enabled her to endure years of mental and emotional struggles, as well as horrible censure and imprisonment by religious authorities.

She was born into a corrupt age, in a nation noted for its immorality, and was taught and raised in a church as decadent as the world around it. She lived and died in the Catholic Church, the same one that strongly rejected many of her beliefs. When church authorities demanded her money and property, she willingly surrendered them, even though she knew it would leave her penniless. She was imprisoned for years, and her only crime was that she loved God.

In the midst of all this, Madame Guyon remained convinced that prayer was purposeful and powerful, the tool that moved God to respond to us. Many of the events of her life taught her to pray with a depth many people never discover. She prayed with a rare and intense fervency, knowing that God alone could bring about the desired changes. Some things were changed in her life; others were not. One thing that did not change was her unshakable faith and belief in the loving Christ. This hope and strength produced in her the character required to endure the life she was handed.

Madame Guyon was one of the main leaders and writers of the seventeenth-century movement known as Quietism, which downplayed the importance of works in religion and emphasized a total surrender to God. After her husband's death, Guyon dedicated herself entirely to Christian ministry. She traveled through the towns of France and Switzerland, reaching out to all segments of society and sharing her insights on how to live a holy life. Hers was not a public ministry, but mainly one of personal evangelism, challenging people to live a holy life by placing their faith in Christ.

Despite all the controversy, her writings won her both Catholic and Protestant admirers in France, Germany, Holland, and England. Consequently, thousands have been drawn into a closer relationship with God by reading of her deep devotion to him. In describing her own writing she said, "My earnest wish is to paint in true colors the goodness of God to me, and the depth of my own ingratitude." This perception of God's great grace, coupled with an acute awareness of her own sinful state, forms the heart of her story.

To see someone like this is rare; to know them is even rarer. Yet through the pages of this excerpt, you'll be able to catch a glimpse into the faith of Madame Guyon as she outlines the importance, the call, and the methods of successful prayer.

*Dave*

# MADAME GUYON
Excerpted from *A Short and Easy Method of Prayer*[10]

## CHAPTER I: THE UNIVERSAL CALL TO PRAYER

Prayer is the application of the heart to GOD, and the internal exercise of love. S. Paul hath enjoined us to *"pray without ceasing"* [1 Thessalonians 5:17], and our Lord saith, *"I say unto you all, watch and pray"* [Mark 13:33, 37]: all therefore may, and all ought to practice prayer. I grant that meditation is attainable but by few, for few are capable of it; and therefore, my beloved brethren who are athirst for salvation, meditative prayer is not the prayer which GOD requires of you, nor which we would recommend.

Let all pray: we should live by prayer, as we should live by love. *"I counsel you to buy of me gold tried in the fire, that ye may be rich"* [Revelation 3:18], this is much more easily obtained than we can conceive. *"Come, all ye that are athirst, to these living waters";* nor lose your precious moments in *"hewing out cisterns, broken cisterns that will hold no water"* [John 7:37; Jeremiah 2:13].

Madame Guyon refers to the *practice* of prayer. Just as any other relationship needs ongoing effort to grow, true communication with God requires consistency and discipline.

Come, ye famished souls, who find naught whereon to feed; come, and ye shall be fully satisfied! Come, ye poor afflicted ones, who groan beneath your load of wretchedness and pain, and ye shall find ease and comfort! Come, ye sick, to your Physician, and be not fearful of approaching Him because ye are filled with diseases; expose them to His view and they shall be healed! All who are desirous of prayer may easily pray, enabled by those ordinary graces and gifts of the HOLY SPIRIT which are common to all men.

Prayer is the guide to perfection and the sovereign good; it delivers us from every vice, and obtains us every virtue; for the one great means to become perfect, is to walk in the presence of GOD: He Himself hath said, *"walk in my presence and be ye perfect"* [Genesis 17:1]. It is by prayer alone, that we are brought into this presence, and maintained in it without interruption.

You must then learn a species of prayer, which may be exercised at all times; which doth not obstruct outward employments; and which may be equally practiced by princes, kings, prelates, priests and magistrates, soldiers and children, tradesmen, labourers, women and sick persons: it cannot, therefore, be the prayer of the head, but of the heart; not a prayer of the understanding alone, which is so limited in its operations that it can have but one object at one time; but the prayer of the heart is not interrupted by the exercises of reason: indeed nothing can interrupt this prayer, but irregular and disordered affections: and when once we have tasted of GOD, and the sweetness of His love, we shall find it impossible to relish aught but Himself?

Nothing is so easily obtained as the possession and enjoyment of GOD, for *"in him we live, move, and have our being;"* and He is more desirous to give Himself into us, than we can be to receive Him.

All consists in the manner of seeking Him; and to seek aright, is easier and more natural to us than breathing. Though you think yourselves ever so stupid, dull, and incapable of sublime attainments, yet, by prayer, you may live in GOD Himself with less difficulty or interruption than you live in the vital air. Will it not then be highly sinful to neglect prayer? But this I trust you will not, when you have learnt the method, which is exceedingly easy.

## CHAPTER II: THE METHOD OF PRAYER

There are two ways of introducing a soul into prayer, which should for some time be pursued; the one is Meditation, the other is Reading accompanied with Meditation.

Meditative Reading is the choosing some important practical or speculative truth, always

Imagine enjoying a prayer life that's active and constant throughout the endless distractions of your daily life. Now *that's* getting to know God!

preferring the practical, and proceeding thus: whatever truth you have chosen, read only a small portion of it, endeavoring to taste and digest it, to extract the essence and substance thereof, and proceed no farther while any savor or relish remains in the passage: when this subsides, take up your book again and proceed as before, seldom reading more than half a page at a time, for it is not the quantity that is read, but the manner of reading, that yields us profit.

Those who read fast reap no more advantage than a bee would by only skimming over the surface of the flower, instead of waiting to penetrate into it, and extract its sweets. Much reading is rather for scholastic subjects than divine truths: indeed, to receive real profit from spiritual books, we must read as I have described; and I am certain, if that method were pursued, we should become gradually habituated to, and more fully disposed for prayer.

Madame Guyon makes an interesting connection between studying divine truths and our prayer life.

Meditation, which is the other method, is to be practiced at an appropriated season, and not in the time of reading. I believe the best manner of meditating is as follows:—When, by an act of lively faith, you are placed in the Presence of GOD, recollect some truth wherein there is substance and food; pause gently and sweetly thereon, not to employ the reason, but merely to calm and fix the mind: for you must observe, that your principal exercise should ever be the Presence of GOD; your subject, therefore, should rather serve to stay the mind, than exercise the understanding.

From this procedure, it will necessarily follow, that the lively faith in a GOD immediately present in our inmost soul, will produce an eager and vehement pressing inwardly into ourselves, and a restraining all our senses from wandering abroad: this serves to extricate us speedily from numberless distractions, to remove us far from external objects, and to bring us nigh unto our GOD, Who is only to be found in our inmost centre, which is the Holy of Holies wherein He dwelleth.

It is proper here to caution beginners against wandering from truth to truth, and from subject to subject: the right way to penetrate every divine truth, to enjoy its full relish, and to imprint it on the heart, is dwelling on it whilst its savor continues.

Though recollection is difficult in the beginning, from the habit the soul has acquired of being always from home; yet, when by the violence it hath done itself, it becometh a little accustomed to it, it will soon be rendered perfectly easy, and become delightful. Such is the experimental taste and sense of His Presence, and such the efficacy of those graces, which that GOD bestows, Whose One Will towards His creatures is to communicate Himself unto them!

## CHAPTER III: THE FIRST DEGREE OF PRAYER

Those who have not learnt to read, are not, on that account, excluded from prayer; for the Great Book which teacheth all things, and which is legible as well internally as externally, is JESUS CHRIST Himself.

The method they should practice is this: They should first learn this fundamental truth, that *"the kingdom of God is within them"* [Luke 17:21], and that it is there, only it must be sought.

It is as incumbent on the Clergy, to instruct their parishioners in prayer, as in their catechism. It is true, they tell them the end of their creation; but should they not also give them sufficient instructions how they may attain it? They should be taught to begin by an act of profound adoration and abasement before GOD; and closing the corporeal eyes, endeavor to open those of the soul: they should then collect themselves inwardly,

According to Madame Guyon, one key to connecting with God through prayer is taking the time to be with him, letting his truths sink into our minds and hearts. God wants to communicate with us, but we must quiet ourselves to hear him.

In this section, Madame Guyon continues her discussion about training our focus on God in order to be truly in his presence. In prayer we can worship God and bring our concerns to him.

and, by a lively faith in GOD, as dwelling within them, pierce into the Divine Presence; not suffering the senses to wander abroad, but withholding them as much as may be in due subjection.

They should then repeat the LORD'S Prayer in their native tongue, pondering a little upon the meaning of the words, and the infinite willingness of that GOD Who dwells within them, to become, indeed, their Father. In this state let them pour out their wants before Him; and when they have pronounced the endearing word, Father, remain a few moments in a respectful silence, waiting to have the will of this their heavenly Father made manifest unto them.

At other times they should place themselves as sheep before their Shepherd, looking up to Him for their true substantial food: "*O Divine Shepherd, Thou feedest Thy flock with Thyself, and art, indeed, their daily nourishment!*" They may also represent unto Him the necessities of their families: but all upon this principle, and in this one great view of faith, that GOD is within them.

The ideas we form of the Divine Being fall infinitely short of what He is: a lively faith in His presence is sufficient: for we must not form any image of the Deity; though we may of the Second Person in the ever-blessed TRINITY, beholding Him in the various states of His Incarnation, from His Birth to His Crucifixion, or in some other state or mystery, provided the soul always seeks for those views in its inmost ground or centre.

When the Divine Presence is granted us, and we gradually relish silence and repose, this experimental feeling and taste of the Presence of GOD introduces the soul into the second degree of prayer, which, by proceeding in the manner I have described, is attainable as well by the illiterate as the learned: some favored souls, indeed, are indulged with it, even from the beginning.

## CHAPTER IV: THE SECOND DEGREE OF PRAYER

SOME call the second degree of prayer, "The Prayer of Contemplation," "The Prayer of Faith and Stillness," and others call it, "The Prayer of Simplicity." I shall here use this latter appellation, as being more just than any of the former, which imply a much more exalted state of prayer than that I am now treating of.

First, as soon as the soul by faith places itself in the Presence of GOD, and becomes recollected before Him, let it remain thus for a little time in a profound and respectful silence.

But if, at the beginning, in forming the act of faith, it feels some little pleasing sense of the Divine Presence; let it remain there without being troubled for a subject, and proceed no farther, but carefully cherish this sensation while it continues: as soon as it abates, the will may be excited by some tender affection; and if by the first moving thereof, it finds itself reinstated in sweet peace, let it there remain: the smothered fire must be gently fanned; but as soon as it is kindled, we must cease that effort, lest we extinguish it by our own activity.

Go then to prayer, not that ye may enjoy spiritual delights, but that ye may be either full or empty, just as it pleaseth GOD: this will preserve you in an evenness of spirit, in desertion as well as in consolation, and prevent your being surprised at aridity or the apparent repulses of GOD.

## CHAPTER V: OF SPIRITUAL ARIDITY

THOUGH GOD hath no other desire than to impart Himself to the loving soul that seeks Him, yet He frequently conceals Himself that the soul may be roused from sloth, and impelled to seek Him with fidelity and love. But with what abundant goodness doth He recompense the faithfulness of His beloved? And how sweetly are these apparent withdrawings of Himself succeeded by the consoling caresses of love?

The more we are in God's presence the more we enjoy it. Yet even more important than seeking our own joy in prayer is the simple pursuit of knowing God more deeply.

Be ye, therefore, patient in prayer, though, during life, you can do naught else than wait the return of the Beloved, in deep humiliation, calm contentment, and patient resignation to His will. And yet how this most

We all go through periods of spiritual dryness when it seems God is far away or we are plagued by apathy. Those who "hang in there" in faith will come through those times with a deeper understanding of God's goodness and grace.

excellent prayer may be intermingled with the sighings of plaintive love! This conduct, indeed, is most pleasing to the heart of JESUS; and, above all others, will, as it were, compel Him to return.

# VITAL STATS

**WHEN AND WHERE:** William Law lived in Cambridge (England) during the eighteenth century.

**STYLE:** William Law is honest and compelling. He doesn't beat around the bush.

**NOTEWORTHY ACCOMPLISHMENT:** William Law's writing helped awaken a generation, including future church leaders such as John and Charles Wesley and George Whitefield, to sincere devotion to Christ.

**TIMELESS WISDOM:** William Law invites believers to live a balanced Christian life, responding to God's grace with willful obedience.

At some point in life we're each hit with a tough situation that feels like we've been dealt a bum rap. That's living—a mix of highs and lows, joys and disappointments. William Law was no stranger to those ups and downs. Born in the village of King's Cliffe in England, Law was educated at Cambridge University with the desire to enter full-time ministry with the Church of England. He was well on his way. But when Law refused to take an oath of allegiance to King George I, he was deprived of the priesthood. It seemed like a rotten deal.

Yet Law seemed to make the most of an unfortunate situation. He became a tutor, and God opened up another platform for preaching: Law began expressing his sermons and messages through books. A few of his works include *Christian Perfection*, *The Way to Divine Knowledge*, and *Spirit of Love*; but his best-known book, *A Serious Call to a Devout and Holy Life*, was published in 1728. In it, he suggests that God doesn't just forgive disobedience, but rather calls followers to obedience to God's Word in every area of life.

The following excerpt from *A Serious Call to a Devout and*

*Holy Life* still echoes of Law's straightforward and compelling style that has made the book one of the most popular in history. Law doesn't mince words. He challenges believers to live wholly for God in everything they do. He encourages followers of Christ to leave behind daily distractions and make their Christianity obvious through their words and actions. At times, Law's words seem sharp, harsh, and even judgmental, but it's also this tone that rings loudly as a wake-up call to those who have settled for a lazy faith.

As the pendulum in church history has swung between emphasizing faith or works, *A Serious Call to a Devout and Holy Life* highlights the importance of showing the world through our actions that living for Jesus really does make a difference in a person's everyday habits.

Whether or not you agree with the fervor of Law's tone, it's tough to come away unchallenged by his words. Many of his contemporaries and those who followed after him—including John and Charles Wesley, George Whitefield, William Wilberforce, and Thomas Scott—have described reading *A Serious Call to a Devout and Holy Life* as a turning point in their lives. Like them, may the following excerpt inspire you in your faith.

*Margaret*

## CHAPTER I

### *What Is Devotion to God?*

Devotion is neither private nor public prayer; but prayers, whether private or public, are particular parts or instances of devotion. Devotion signifies a life given, or devoted, to God.

> In this opening section, Law defines what it means to be devoted to God.

He, therefore, is the devout man, who lives no longer to his own will, or the way and spirit of the world, but to the sole will of God; who considers God in everything, who serves God in everything, who makes all the parts of his common life parts of piety, by doing everything in the Name of God, and under such rules as are conformable to His glory. We readily acknowledge that God alone is to be the rule and measure of our prayers; that in them we are to look wholly unto Him, and act wholly for Him; that we are only to pray in such a manner, for such things, and such ends, as are suitable to His glory.

Now let any one but find out the reason why he is to be thus strictly pious in his prayers, and he will find the same as strong a reason to be as strictly pious in all the other parts of his life. For there is not the least shadow of a reason why we should make God the rule and measure of our prayers; why we should then look wholly unto Him, and pray according to His will; but what equally proves it necessary for us to look wholly unto God, and make Him the rule and measure of all the other actions of our life.

> Law believes God should not only be the center of everything, but he should also be the circumference as well, enveloping every part of our existence.

For any ways of life, any employment of our talents, whether of our parts, our time, or money, that is not strictly according to the will of God, that is not for such ends as are suitable to His glory, are as great absurdities and failings, as prayers that are not according to the will of God. For there is no other reason why our prayers should be according to the will of God, why they should have nothing in them but what is wise, and holy, and heavenly; there is no other reason for this, but that our lives may be of the same nature, full of the same wisdom, holiness, and heavenly tempers, that we may live unto God in the same spirit that we pray unto Him. Were it not our strict duty to live by reason, to devote all the actions of our lives to God, were it not absolutely necessary to walk before Him in wisdom and holiness and all heavenly conversation, doing everything in His Name, and for His glory, there would be no excellency or wisdom in the most heavenly prayers. Nay, such prayers would be absurdities; they would be like prayers for wings, when it was no part of our duty to fly. . . .

Law speaks out against those who just pretend to be Christian. If we're going to pray like true believers, we need to act like true believers.

It is for want of knowing, or at least considering this, that we see such a mixture of ridicule in the lives of many people. You see them strict as to some times and places of devotion, but when the service of the Church is over, they are but like those that seldom or never come there. In their way of life, their manner of spending their time and money, in their cares and fears, in their pleasures and indulgences, in their labour and diversions, they are like the rest of the world. This makes the loose part of the world generally make a jest of those that are devout, because they see their devotion goes no farther than their prayers, and that when they are over, they live no more unto God, till the time of prayer returns again; but live by the same humour and fancy, and in as full an enjoyment of all the follies of life as other people. This is the reason why they are the jest and scorn of careless and worldly people; not because they are really devoted to God, but because they appear to have no other devotion but that of occasional prayers.

### Recognize the "Julius" Life?

Julius is very fearful of missing prayers; all the parish supposes Julius to be sick, if he is not at Church. But if you were to ask him why he spends the rest of his time by humour or chance? why he is a companion of the silliest people in their most silly pleasures? why he is ready for every impertinent entertainment and diversion? If you were to ask him why there is no amusement too trifling to please him? why he is busy at all balls and assemblies? why he gives himself up to an idle, gossiping conversation? why he lives in foolish friendships and fondness for particular persons, that neither want nor deserve any particular kindness? why he allows himself in foolish hatreds and resentments against particular persons without considering that he is to love everybody as himself?

> It's amazing how tempting it is to live out a Julius-type faith.

If you ask him why he never puts his conversation, his time, and fortune, under the rules of religion? Julius has no more to say for himself than the most disorderly person. For the whole tenor of Scripture lies as directly against such a life, as against debauchery and intemperance: he that lives such a course of idleness and folly, lives no more according to the religion of Jesus Christ, than he that lives in gluttony and intemperance.

If a man was to tell Julius that there was no occasion for so much constancy at prayers, and that he might, without any harm to himself, neglect the service of the Church, as the generality of people do, Julius would think such a one to be no Christian, and that he ought to avoid his company. But if a person only tells him, that he may live as the generality of the world does, that he may enjoy himself as others do, that he may spend his time and money as people of fashion do, that he may conform to the follies and frailties of the generality, and gratify his tempers and passions as most people do, Julius never suspects that man to want a Christian spirit, or that he is doing the devil's work. And if Julius was to read all the New Testament from the beginning to the end, he would find his course of life condemned in every page of it.

Law takes a harsh tone with Julius-type people, but bases his words on the Bible's teachings in the New Testament.

And indeed there cannot anything be imagined more absurd in itself, than wise, and sublime, and heavenly prayers, added to a life of vanity and folly, where neither labour nor diversions, neither time nor money, are under the direction of the wisdom and heavenly tempers of our prayers. If we were to see a man pretending to act wholly with regard to God in everything that he did, that would neither spend time nor money, nor take any labour or diversion, but so far as he could act according to strict principles of reason and piety, and yet at the same time neglect all prayer, whether public or private, should we not be amazed at such a man, and wonder how he could have so much folly along with so much religion?

Yet this is as reasonable as for any person to pretend to strictness in devotion, to be careful of observing times and places of prayer, and yet letting the rest of his life, his time and labour, his talents and money, be disposed of without any regard to strict rules of piety and devotion. For it is as great an absurdity to suppose holy prayers, and Divine petitions, without a holiness of life suitable to them, as to suppose a holy and Divine life without prayers.

Let any one therefore think how easily he could confute a man that pretended to great strictness of life without prayer, and the same arguments will as plainly confute another, that pretends to strictness of prayer, without carrying the same strictness into every other part of life. For to be weak and foolish in spending our time and fortune, is no greater a mistake, than to be weak and foolish in relation to our prayers. And to allow ourselves in any ways of life that neither are, nor can be offered to God, is the same irreligion, as to neglect our prayers, or use them in such a manner as make them an offering unworthy of God. . . .

Law does not equate church attendance with authentic faith.

### What about Church?

It is very observable, that there is not one command in all the Gospel for public worship; and perhaps it is a duty that is least insisted upon in Scripture of any other. The frequent attendance at it is never so much as mentioned in all the New Testament. Whereas that religion or devotion which is to govern the ordinary actions of our life is to be found in almost every verse of Scripture. Our blessed Saviour and His Apostles are wholly taken up in doctrines that relate to common life. They call us to renounce the world, and differ in every temper and way of life, from the spirit and the way of the world: to renounce all its goods, to fear none of its evils, to reject its joys, and have no value for its happiness: to be as new-born babes, that are born into a new state of things: to live as pilgrims in spiritual watching, in holy fear, and heavenly aspiring after another life: to take up our daily cross, to deny ourselves, to profess the blessedness of mourning, to seek the blessedness of poverty of spirit: to forsake the pride and vanity of riches, to take no thought for the morrow, to live in the profoundest state of humility, to rejoice in worldly sufferings: to reject the lust of the flesh, the lust of the eyes, and the pride of life: to bear injuries, to forgive and bless our enemies, and to love mankind as God loveth them: to give up our whole hearts and affections to God, and strive to enter through the strait gate into a life of eternal glory.

This is the common devotion which our blessed Saviour taught, in order to make it the common life of all Christians. Is it not therefore exceeding strange that people should place so much piety in the attendance upon public worship, concerning which there is not one precept of our Lord's to be found, and yet neglect these common duties of our ordinary life, which are commanded in every page of the Gospel? I call these duties the devotion of our common life, because if they are to be practised, they must be made parts of our common life; they can have no place anywhere else. . . .

Thus it is in all the virtues and holy tempers of Christianity; they are not ours unless they be the virtues and tempers of our ordinary life. So that Christianity is so far from leaving us to live in the common ways of life, conforming to the folly of customs, and gratifying the passions and tempers which the spirit of the world delights in, it is so far from indulging us in any

Law calls us to live out our faith in the ordinary.

of these things, that all its virtues which it makes necessary to salvation are only so many ways of living above and contrary to the world, in all the common actions of our life. If our common life is not a common course of humility, self-denial, renunciation of the world, poverty of spirit, and heavenly affection, we do not live the lives of Christians.

# VITAL STATS

**WHEN AND WHERE:** Although born and raised in England, Charles Wesley ended up having a great reach in the United States during the eighteenth century.

**STYLE:** Charles Wesley was a traveling evangelist. His goal was to reach as many people as he could with the gospel of Jesus. Unlike many evangelists of his time, he had a very gentle, emotional side to him. He loved poetry, songwriting, and the arts.

**NOTEWORTHY ACCOMPLISHMENTS:** He played a major role in the formulation of the Methodist church and wrote approximately six thousand hymns.

**TIMELESS WISDOM:** Charles Wesley's lifelong message reminds us that all of life and eternity hinges on Christ. It's still all about Jesus.

Whether you know much about him or not, you've probably at least heard of Charles Wesley. Wesley was a Christian champion of his time. As well-known and very loved preachers, he and his brother John were quite influential for the cause of Christianity during the eighteenth century here in the United States and abroad in their homeland of England. Their theology, preaching, and hard work laid the foundation of the Methodist church in the Americas—one of the largest religious denominations in the United States.

Many people were first introduced to Charles Wesley through his church hymns, which are rich in poetry, depth, and rhythm. Wesley wrote hymns throughout his lifetime, many of which still grace the pages of contemporary hymnals and praise-and-worship booklets. Churches all over the world still sing some of Wesley's more famous songs. In fact, "Christ the Lord Is Risen Today" is a staple every Easter Sunday. And, of course, millions around the world have sung his famous Christmas carol "Hark! The Herald Angels Sing" for more than two centuries.

Many theologians and cultural analysts have named Wesley one of the greatest hymn writers ever and have compared him to other famous hymn writers like Isaac Watts and Fanny Crosby. Wesley is believed to have written more than six thousand hymns in his lifetime.

Theologians and seminary professors today still value Wesley's love of Scripture and theology. They're intrigued by his desire to know truth and reveal that truth through so many facets of media—songs, sermons, classroom lecture, and books. In seminary classes all over the world, students study his influence on American spirituality. New theologians are beginning to realize the grand scope of Wesley's influential offerings to modern theology. During Wesley's lifetime, his powerful presence and delivery challenged the dominant reformed theology beliefs of predestination, election, and limited atonement (see John Calvin's excerpt, page 40). He urged Christians to believe in humanity's free will to choose God and the power of eternal choice. Although some disagree with his beliefs, no one can belittle the impact he has had on many generations.

However, possibly more influential than his theology were his sermons that convicted a generation to turn away from its evil and self-centered ways and choose a life of following Jesus. He and his brother together were an integral part of the reason America experienced a spiritual revolution of sorts in the 1700s called the Great Awakening. Wesley's message was all about awakening.

His thoughts about faith penetrated the hearts of thousands while he was alive. His messages were convicting and soul-stirring. However, he was surprisingly not known for his eloquence in speaking. In fact, his sermons were somewhat cumbersome and unrefined.

In his sermon "Awake, Thou That Sleepest," his words inspire the soul to come out of its slumber and be awakened by the light of Jesus Christ. As you'll read below, even his message outlines were simple and somewhat unimaginative. Yet this excerpt reminds us that our only chance for spiritual survival from sin's hold is found when we run into the light of Christ. Enjoy.

*Matthew*

# CHARLES WESLEY

Excerpted from "Awake, Thou That Sleepest"[12]
Preached on Sunday, April 4, 1742, before the University of Oxford

### Defining Sleep

*Awake, thou that sleepest, and arise from the dead, and Christ shall give thee light.*

Ephesians 5:14

In discoursing on these words, I shall, with the help of God, —First. Describe the sleepers, to whom they are spoken: Secondly. Enforce the exhortation, "Awake, thou that sleepest, and arise from the dead:"

> Ephesians 5:14 is certainly a powerful verse to build a sermon on.

## I

1. And first, as to the sleepers here spoken to. By sleep is signified the natural state of man; that deep sleep of the soul, into which the sin of Adam hath cast all who spring from his loins: That supiness, indolence, and stupidity, that insensibility of his real condition, wherein every man comes Into the world, and continues till the voice of God awakes him.

2. Now, "they that sleep, sleep in the night." The state of nature is a state of utter darkness; a state wherein "darkness covers the earth, and gross darkness the people." The poor unawakened sinner, how much knowledge soever he may have as to other things, has no knowledge of himself: in this respect "he knoweth nothing yet as he ought to know." He knows not that he is a fallen spirit, whose only business in the present world, is to recover

> Wesley gets right to his point. There's no interesting story to open things up; he simply tells you the point of his sermon and then proceeds to back up his point with Scripture.

from his fall, to regain that image of God wherein he was created. He sees *no necessity* for the *one thing needful*, even that inward universal change, that "birth from above," figured out by baptism, which is the beginning of that total renovation. that sanctification of spirit, soul, and body, "without which no man shall see the Lord."

*Wesley eloquently points out the desperate state of humanity before God is revealed.*

3. Full of all diseases as he is, he fancies himself in perfect health. Fast bound in misery and iron, he dreams that he is at liberty. He says, "Peace! Peace!" while the devil, as "a strong, man armed," is in full possession of his soul. He sleeps on still and takes his rest, though hell is moved from beneath to meet him; though the pit from whence there is no return hath opened its mouth to swallow him up. A fire is kindled around him, yet he knoweth it not; yea, it burns him, yet he lays it not to heart.

4. By one who sleeps, we are, therefore, to understand (and would to God we might all understand it!) a sinner satisfied in his sins; contented to remain in his fallen state, to live and die without the image of God; one who is ignorant both of his disease, and of the only remedy for it; one who never was warned, or never regarded the warning voice of God, "to flee from the wrath to come;" one that never yet saw he was in danger of hell-fire, or cried out in the earnestness of his soul, "What must I do to be saved?"

### Sleeping in Oblivion and Hypocrisy

*It's one thing to be lost; it's even worse to be oblivious to it.*

5. If this sleeper be not outwardly vicious, his sleep is usually the deepest of all: whether he be of the Laodicean spirit, "neither cold nor hot," but a quiet, rational, inoffensive, good-natured professor of the religion of his fathers; or whether he be zealous and orthodox, and, "after the most straitest sect of our religion," live "a Pharisee;" that is, according to the scriptural account, one that justifies himself; one that labours to establish his own righteousness, as the ground of his acceptance with God.

6. This is he, who, "having a form of godliness, denies the power thereof;"

yea, and probably reviles it, wheresoever it is found, as mere extravagance and delusion. Meanwhile, the wretched self-deceiver thanks God, that he is "not as other men are; adulterers, unjust, extortioners": no, he doeth no wrong to any man. He "fasts twice in a week," uses all the means of grace, is constant at church and sacrament, yea, and "gives tithes of all that he has;" does all the good that he can "touching the righteousness of the law," he is "blameless": he wants nothing of godliness, but the power; nothing of religion, but the spirit; nothing of Christianity, but the truth and the life.

7. But know ye not, that, however highly esteemed among men such a Christian as this may be, he is an abomination in the sight of God, and an heir of every woe which the Son of God, yesterday, to-day, and for ever, denounces against "scribes and Pharisees, hypocrites"? he hath "made clean the outside of the cup and the platter," but within is full of all filthiness. "An evil disease cleaveth still unto him, so that his inward parts are very wickedness." . . .

8. This is another character of the sleeper here spoken to. He abides in death, though he knows it not. He is dead unto God, "dead in trespasses and sins." For, "to be carnally minded is death " Even as it is written, "By one man sin entered into the world, and death by sin; and so death passed upon all men;" not only temporal death, but likewise spiritual and eternal. "In that day that thou eatest," said God to Adam, "thou shalt surely die;" not bodily (unless as he then became mortal), but spiritually: thou shalt lose the life of thy soul; thou shalt die to God: shalt be separated from him, thy essential life and happiness.

> Wesley defines many who claim to be Christians as those who say the right words and do the right things, but don't have a true heart for God. His description of the hypocritical "self-deceiver" can certainly be found in our churches today.

### The Pre-Awakening Call

9. Thus first was dissolved the vital union of our soul with God; insomuch that "in the midst of" natural "life, we are" now in spiritual "death." And

As Wesley continues to talk about what a person is like before his awakening, notice his lack of personal story. He preaches his interpretation of the Bible, and that's pretty much it. There's no glamour, but it's still just as powerful and relevant.

herein we remain till the Second Adam [Jesus] becomes a quickening Spirit to us; till he raises the dead, the dead in sin, in pleasure, riches or honours. But, before any dead soul can live, he "hears" (hearkens to) "the voice of the Son of God": he is made sensible of his lost estate, and receives the sentence of death in himself. [H]e knows himself to be "dead while he liveth;" dead to God, and all the things of God; having no more power to perform the actions of a living Christian, than a dead body to perform the functions of a living man.

10. And most certain it is, that one dead in sin has not "senses exercised to discern spiritual good and evil." "Having eyes, he sees not; he hath ears, and hears not." He doth not "taste and see that the Lord is gracious." He "hath not seen God at any time," nor "heard his voice," nor "handled the word of life." . . .

11. And hence, having no spiritual senses, no inlets of spiritual knowledge, the natural man receiveth not the things of the Spirit of God; nay, he is so far from receiving them, that whatsoever is spiritually discerned is mere foolishness unto him. He is not content with being utterly ignorant of spiritual things, but he denies the very existence of them. And spiritual sensation itself is to him the foolishness of folly. "How," saith he, "can these things be? How can any man *know* that he is alive to God?" Even as you know that your body is now alive. Faith is the life of the soul; and if ye have this life abiding in you, ye want no marks to evidence it *to yourself*, but *elegchos pneumatos*, that divine consciousness, that *witness* of God, which is more and greater than ten thousand human witnesses.

12. If he doth not now bear witness with thy spirit, that thou art a child of God, O that he might convince thee, thou poor unawakened sinner, by his demonstration and power, that thou art a child of the devil! O that, as I prophesy, there might now be "a noise and a shaking;" and may "the bones

come together, bone to his bone!" Then "come from the four winds, O Breath! and breathe on these slain, that they may live!" And do not ye harden your hearts, and resist the Holy Ghost, who even now is come to convince you of sin, "because you believe not on the name of the only begotten Son of God."

We can't truly understand how lost we are until God awakens his truth in us.

### The Call of God

II

1. Wherefore, "awake, thou that sleepest, and arise from the dead." God calleth thee now by my mouth; and bids thee know thyself, thou fallen spirit, thy true state and only concern below. "What meanest thou, O sleeper? Arise! Call upon thy God, if so be thy God will think upon thee, that thou perish not." A mighty tempest is stirred up round about thee, and thou art sinking into the depths of perdition, the gulf of God's judgments. If thou wouldest escape them, cast thyself into them. "Judge thyself, and thou shalt not be judged of the Lord."

2. Awake, awake! Stand up this moment, lest thou "drink at the Lord's hand the cup of his fury." Stir up thyself to lay hold on the Lord, the Lord thy Righteousness, mighty to save! "Shake thyself from the dust." At least, let the earth-

It is here where Wesley's words take a powerful turn. He stops talking about the desolate soul of man and begins to speak of the power and forgiveness and redemption found in Jesus. Still, his words are harsh.

quake of God's threatenings shake thee. Awake, and cry out with the trembling jailer, "What must I do to be saved?" And never rest till thou believest on the Lord Jesus, with a faith, which is his gift, by the operation of his Spirit. . . .

4. O may the Angel of the Lord come upon thee, and the light shine into thy prison! And mayest thou feel the stroke of an Almighty Hand, raising

thee, with, "Arise up quickly, gird thyself, and bind on thy sandals, cast thy garment about thee, and follow Me."

5. Awake, thou everlasting spirit, out of thy dream of worldly happiness! Did not God create thee for himself? Then thou canst not rest till thou restest in him. Return, thou wanderer! Fly back to thy ark, this is not thy home. Think not of building tabernacles here. Thou art but a stranger, a sojourner upon earth; a creature of a day, but just launching out into an unchangeable state. Make haste. Eternity is at hand. Eternity depends on this moment. An eternity of happiness, or an eternity of misery!

6. In what state is thy soul? Was God, while I am yet speaking, to require it of thee, art thou ready to meet death and judgement? Canst thou stand in his sight, who is of "purer eyes than to behold iniquity"? Art thou "meet to be partaker of the inheritance of the saints in light"? Hast thou "fought a good fight, and kept the faith"? Hast thou secured the one thing needful? Hast thou recovered the image of God, even righteousness and true holiness? Hast thou put off the old man, and put on the new? Art thou clothed upon with Christ?

> We forget that we are just passing through this world. We hold on to things so tightly. All of us can take that sermon to heart!

7. Hast thou oil in thy lamp? Grace in thy heart? Dost thou "love the Lord thy God with all thy heart, and with all thy mind and with all thy soul, and with all thy strength"? Is that mind in thee, which was also in Christ Jesus? Art thou a Christian indeed, that is, a new creature? Are old things passed away, and all things become new?

8. Art thou a "partaker of the divine nature"? Knowest thou not, that "Christ is in thee, except thou be reprobate"? Knowest thou, that God "dwelleth in thee, and thou in God, by his Spirit, which he hath given thee"? Knowest thou not that "thy body is a temple of the Holy Ghost, which thou hast of God"? Hast thou the witness in thyself? the earnest of thine inheritance? Hast thou "received the Holy Ghost"? Or dost thou start at the question, not knowing "whether there be any Holy Ghost"? . . .

10. Yet, on the authority of God's Word, and our own Church, I must repeat the question, "Hast thou received the Holy Ghost?" If thou hast not, thou art not yet a Christian. For a Christian is a man that is "anointed with the Holy Ghost and with power." Thou art not yet made a partaker of pure religion and undefiled. Dost thou know what religion is?—that it is a participation of the divine nature; the life of God in the soul of man; Christ formed in the heart; "Christ in thee, the hope of glory;". . .

12. Thou hopest to be saved; but what reason hast thou to give of the hope that is in thee? Is it because thou hast done no harm? Or, because thou hast done much good? Or, because thou art not like other men; but wise, or learned, or honest, and morally good; esteemed of men, and of a fair reputation? Alas! all this will never bring thee to God. It is in his account lighter than vanity. Dost thou know Jesus Christ, whom he hath sent? Hath he taught thee, that "by grace we are saved through faith; and that not of ourselves: it is the gift of God: not of works, lest any man should boast"? Hast thou received the faithful saying as the whole foundation of thy hope, "that Jesus Christ came into the world to save sinners"? Hast thou learned what that meaneth? . . .

13. O that in all these questions ye may hear the voice that wakes the dead; and feel that hammer of the Word, which breaketh the rocks in pieces! "If ye will hear his voice to-day, while it is called to-day, harden not your hearts." Now, "awake, thou that sleepest" in spiritual death, that thou sleep not in death eternal! Feel thy lost estate, and "arise from the dead." Leave thine old companions in sin and death. Follow thou Jesus, and let the dead bury their dead. "Save thyself from this untoward generation." "Come out from among them, and be thou separate, and touch not the unclean thing, and the Lord shall receive thee." "Christ shall give thee light."

Wesley ends his words with a resounding, "Christ will give you light!" All of us need the light of God. We need it to see. We need it to hear. We need it to live. Not one of us can walk through the darkness of the world without the light of God.

# VITAL STATS

**WHEN AND WHERE:** He was influential during the Great Awakening, preaching revival sermons throughout the United Kingdom and America. Although he was a contemporary and good friend of John and Charles Wesley, his reformed, Calvinist theology differed from theirs. (See previous excerpts of John Calvin and Charles Wesley, pages 40 and 99.)

**STYLE:** George Whitefield's passionate speaking style appealed to the masses, as well as to the intellects. Evangelical fervor characterized his sermons, often resulting in rejection from more conservative, traditionalist preachers.

**NOTEWORTHY ACCOMPLISHMENT:** Starting at age twenty-two, he preached more than eighteen-thousand sermons in his life, an average of five hundred a year or ten a week.

**TIMELESS WISDOM:** Christ longs to share with you, his bride, an intimacy and love beyond your wildest dreams.

A voice booms through the auditorium with such force the windows rattle in protest. Throngs of listeners jostle for a better view of the stage. The energy is palpable, the beat pulses through your veins.

It may sound like a U2 concert, but it's actually the scene at an eighteenth-century church in the English countryside, and the speaker is a young preacher named George Whitefield.

Maybe you've heard of a time known as the Great Awakening, but you're not sure what it was, or you haven't really cared. George Whitefield was a key player in this era that transformed Christian history. Let me introduce you to this mighty speaker.

When young Whitefield grew tired of the lifeless sermons of his day, he decided to bring new energy to countless churchgoers by offering them a picture of a personal relationship with Jesus the Savior. Whitefield often clashed with traditionalists who did not welcome any change to their spiritual diet and was even barred from continuing to preach in some churches. Yet his words were a breath of life for countless others seeking a genuine touch of biblical hope.

With tireless zeal, Whitefield preached thousands of sermons, averaging ten per week over his lifetime. His words of truth captivated audiences throughout England as well as in the English colonies across the Atlantic.

His message may be hundreds of years old, but it is as fresh today as it was when he spoke it. Rediscover along with him the wonder of being Christ's cherished bride. It's time for another Great Awakening, and we're just the generation to live out the next story in God's epic!

*Janella*

### The Most Amazing Relationship

"For thy Maker is thy Husband." Isaiah 54:5, ASV

Although believers by nature, are far from God, and children of wrath, even as others, yet it is amazing to think how nigh they are brought to him again by the blood of Jesus Christ. Eye hath not seen, nor ear heard, neither hath it entered into the heart of any man living, fully to conceive, the nearness and dearness of that relation, in which they stand to their common head. He is not ashamed to call them brethren.

Kind and endearing applications these, that undoubtedly bespeak a very near and ineffably intimate union between the Lord Jesus and the true living members of his mystical body! But, methinks, the words of our text point out to us a relation, which not only comprehends, but in respect to nearness and dearness, exceeds all other relations whatsoever. I mean that of a Husband, "For thy Maker is thy husband; the Lord of Hosts is his name; and thy Redeemer the Holy One of Israel, the God of the whole earth shall he be called."

It may not be amiss to consider, what is necessary to be done, before a marriage between two parties amongst ourselves, can be said to be valid in the sight of God and men. And that will lead us in a familiar way, to show what must be done, or what must pass between us and Jesus Christ, before we can say, "our Maker is our husband."

### Prep-work for the Wedding

And *First*, in all lawful marriages, it is absolutely necessary, that the parties to be joined together in that holy and honorable estate, are actually and legally freed from all pre-engagements whatsoever. "A woman is bound to her husband, (saith the apostle) so long as her husband liveth."

Now, it is just thus between us and the Lord Jesus. For, we are all by nature born under, and wedded to the law, as a covenant of works.

But before we can say, "our Maker is our husband," we must be delivered from our old husband the law; we must renounce our own righteousness, our own doings and performances, in point of dependence, whether in whole or part, as dung and dross, for the excellency of the knowledge of Christ Jesus our Lord. For thus speaks the apostle Paul to the Romans, chapter 7:4, "Ye also are become dead to the law (as a covenant of works) by the body of Christ, that ye should be married to another, even to him, who is raised from the dead." As he also speaketh in another place, "I have espoused you, as a chaste virgin to Jesus Christ."

> Some people may feel strange thinking of themselves as the bride of Christ. But that's what he calls his Church. It is the closest kind of relationship and sets the example for deep and sacrificial love.

But further; before a marriage among us can stand good in law, both parties must not only be freed from all pre-engagements, but there must be a mutual consent on both sides.

Before we are actually married or united to him by faith; or, to keep to the terms of the text, before we assuredly can say, that "our Maker is our husband," we must be made willing people in the day of God's power, we must be sweetly and effectually persuaded by the Holy Spirit of God, that the glorious Emanuel is willing to accept of us, just as we are, and also that we are willing to accept of him upon his own terms, yea, upon any terms. And when once it comes to this, the spiritual marriage goes on apace, and there is but one thing lacking to make it complete. And what is that? An actual union.

Some indeed, I am afraid, are so presumptuous as to affirm, as least to insinuate, that there is no such thing as knowing, or being fully assured, whilst here below, whether we are in Christ or not. Or at least, if there be such a thing, it is very rare, or was only the privilege of the primitive believers. Part of this is true, and part of this absolutely false. That this glorious privilege of a full assurance [that we are in Christ] is very rare, is too, too true. And so it is equally too true, that real Christians, comparatively speaking, are very rare also.

### Radiance and Joy

How shall I set forth thy happiness, O believer, thou bride of God! And is thy Maker thy husband? Is his name "The Lord of hosts?" Whom then shouldst thou fear? And is thy Redeemer the holy one of Israel? The God of the whole earth should he be called! Of whom then shouldst thou be afraid? He that toucheth thee, toucheth the very apple of God's eye.

All hail, (I must again repeat it) thou Lamb's bride! For thou art all glorious within, and comely, through the comeliness thy heavenly bridegroom hath put upon thee. Thy garment is indeed of wrought gold; and, ere long, the King shall bring thee forth with a raiment of needle-work, and present thee blameless before his Father, without spot, or wrinkle, or any such thing.

In the mean while, well shall it be with you, and happy shall you be, who are married to Jesus Christ: for all that Christ has, is yours. "He is made of God to you, wisdom, righteousness, sanctification, and eternal redemption." "Whether Paul, or Cephas, or the world, or life, or death, or things present, or things to come; all are yours." All his attributes are engaged for your preservation, and all things shall work together for your good, who love God, and, by being thus married to the Lord Jesus, give an evident proof that you are called according to his purpose.

What say you? When you meditate on these things, are you not frequently ready to cry out, What shall we render unto the Lord for all these mercies, which, of his free unmerited grace, he hath been pleased to bestow upon us? For, though you are dead to the law, as a covenant of works, yet you are alive to the law as a rule of life, and are

> Just as a bride's white gown signifies purity, so does the garment of gold Whitefield mentions. Jesus prepares his followers for the great wedding day when he will be re-united with his bride—the Church.

in, or under the law (for either expression seems to denote the same thing) to your glorious husband, Jesus Christ.

### Living as Christ's Bride

Pass we on therefore to the *second* general head, under which I was to show, what duties of love they owe to Jesus Christ, who are so happy as to be able to say, "My Maker is my husband."

I say, duties of love. For being now married to Jesus Christ, you work not for life, but from life. The love of God constrains you, so that, if there was no written law, or supposing Jesus would set you at liberty from his yoke, so far as grace prevails in your hearts, you would say, we love our blessed bridegroom, and will not go from him.

*In this section, Whitefield explains what is required of the bride of Christ.*

And what does the Lord require of you? That we may speak on this head as plainly as may be, we shall pursue the method we began with; and, by carrying on the allegory, and examining what is required of truly Christian wives, under the gospel, infer what our Lord may justly demand of those who are united to him by faith, and can therefore say, "our Maker is our husband."

And here let us go to the law and to the testimony. What says the scripture? "Let the wife see that she *reverence* her husband."

Does the apostle say, "Let the wife see that she reverence her husband?" May I not pertinently apply this caution to you who are married to Jesus Christ? See to it that you reverence and respect your husband. I say, *see to it*. For the devil will be often suggesting to you hard and mean thoughts against your husband.

*A Christian's entire life centers on bringing glory to Jesus. What a privilege and a challenge!*

Farther, what says the apostle in his epistle to the Ephesians? Speaking of the marriage state, he says, "The wife is the glory of her husband;" as though he had said, a Christian wife should so behave, and so walk, as to be a credit to her husband.

This is to be a help-meet indeed. Such a woman will be praised in the gate; and her husband get glory, and meet with respect on her account. And ought a woman to be the glory of her husband?

How much more ought you, that are the Lamb's bride, so to live, and so to walk, as to bring glory, and gain respect, to the cause and interest of your husband Jesus? This is what the apostle everywhere supposes, when he would draw a parallel between a temporal and spiritual marriage. "The woman, is the glory of her husband, even as the church is the glory of Christ." Agreeable to this, he tells the Corinthians, "Whether you eat or drink, or whatsoever you do, do all to the glory of God;" and as he also speaks to the Thessalonians, 1 Thess. 2:11–12, "As you know how we exhorted, and comforted, and charged every one of you (as a father doth his children) that you would walk worthy of God who hath called you to his kingdom, and his glory." What an expression is here! "That you would walk worthy of God." O! how ought this, and such like texts, to stir up your pure minds, O believers, so to have your conversation in this world, that you may be what the apostle says some particular persons were, even "the glory of Christ." You are his glory; he rejoices over you with singing; and you should so walk, that all who know and hear of you, may glorify Christ in you.

*Subjection*, is another duty, that is enjoined married women, in the word of God. They are to "be subject to their own husbands in every thing." Every lawful thing: "For, the husband is the head of the wife, even as Christ is the head of the church."

And if women are to be subject to their own husbands in every thing, how much more ought believers, whether men or women, to be subject to Jesus Christ: for he is the head of the church. He has bought her by his blood. Believers therefore are not their own, but are under the highest

The idea of *subjection* or *submission* is not a popular one throughout general society. However, this high calling is also a great joy because of the sweetness of serving Jesus.

obligations to glorify and obey Jesus Christ, in their bodies and their souls, which are his.

Add to this, that his service, as it is admirably expressed in one of our collects, is perfect freedom. His commandments holy, just, and good. And therefore it is your highest privilege, O believers, to submit to, and obey them. Earthly husbands may be so mean as to impose some things upon their wives, merely to show their authority; but it is not so with Jesus Christ. He can and does impose nothing, but what immediately conduces to our present, as well as future good.

*Fruitfulness* was a blessing promised by God to the first happy pair; "Increase and multiply, and replenish the earth." "Lo, children, and the fruit of the womb, (says the Psalmist) are a gift and heritage, which cometh of the Lord." And so, if we are married to Jesus Christ, we must be fruitful. In what? In every good word and work: for this speaks the Apostle, in his epistle to the Romans: "Wherefore, my brethren, ye also are become dead to the law, by the body of Christ, that ye should be married to another, even to him who is raised from the dead." What follows? "That we should bring forth fruit unto God."

Once more. Persons that are married, take one another *for better or for worse*, for richer or for poorer, to love and to cherish each other in sickness and in health. And if we are married to Jesus Christ, we shall be willing to bear his *cross*, as well as to wear his *crown*. "If any man will come after me, let him deny himself, take up his cross, and follow me." Neither will they be compelled to do this, as Simon of Cyrene was, but they will be volunteers in his service; they will cry out, Crown him, crown him, when others are crying out, "Crucify him, crucify him." They will never leave or forsake him, but willingly follow the Captain of their salvation, though it be through a sea of blood.

### Your Wedding Invitation
Abraham's faithful servant behaved, when sent out to fetch a wife for his master Isaac. He spake of the riches and honors, which God had conferred

on him; but what infinitely greater honors and riches, has the God and Father of our Lord Jesus, conferred on his only Son, to whom I now invite every Christless sinner! To you, therefore, I call, O ye sons of men, assuring you, there is everything in Jesus that your hearts can desire, or hunger and thirst after.

Do people in disposing of themselves or their children in marriage, generally covet to be matched with *persons of great names*? Let this consideration serve as a motive to stir you up to match with Jesus. For God the Father has given him a name above every name; he has upon his vesture, and upon his thigh, a name written, "The King of kings, and the Lord of lords." Nor has he an empty title, but power equivalent; for he is a prince, as well as savior.

Nor is his *beauty* inferior to his wisdom or holiness; the seraphs veil their faces, when they appear before him: "He is the chiefest among ten thousand, nay, he is altogether lovely." And, as he is altogether lovely, so is he altogether *loving*: his name and his nature is Love. God, God in Christ is love: love in the abstract.

The role of being Christ's bride is not to be taken lightly. It's the most important role we could possibly choose. And there's no way of knowing its fullness without diving in and experiencing Jesus and his promises.

And now . . . shall I put that question to you, which Rebecca's relations, upon a proposal of marriage, put to her? "Will ye go with the man?" With the God-man, this infinitely great, this infinitely powerful, this all-wise, all-holy, altogether lovely, ever-loving Jesus? What objection have you to make against such a gracious offer?

# VITAL STATS

**WHEN AND WHERE:** Frederick Douglass was born into slavery in Maryland, sent to a plantation to work, and eventually escaped. Living many of his adult years in Rochester, New York, he played a key role in recruiting African Americans for the Union Army during the Civil War and worked toward Reconstruction afterward.

**STYLE:** Frederick Douglass's straightforward eloquence raised international attention to the brutality and evils of slavery, as well as to what it truly means to be free.

**NOTEWORTHY ACCOMPLISHMENT:** He was one of history's greatest abolitionists. Douglass's personal relationship with Lincoln helped make emancipation one of the reasons for the Civil War.

**TIMELESS WISDOM:** Frederick Douglass recognized that "without a struggle there can be no progress." Rather than just enjoy personal freedom after escaping from slavery, he used his gifts and talents to help set thousands of others free.

If enduring unspeakable abuse, hunger, separation from loved ones, and denial of any control over his own life had been enough to destroy Frederick Douglass's spirit, then the United States might still be waging internal war over issues of slavery.

If two decades of bondage to other men's whims were a price to be paid for a platform to speak from, then Frederick Douglass paid dearly for his rise to national status and influence.

If scars from countless beatings were an indication of his determination to see his race enjoy basic human freedoms, then Douglass wore his ambitions across his back.

The arena of suffering is a harsh environment, but it does breed deep passion and courage in souls who refuse to give up.

Frederick Augustus Washington Bailey was born to a

slave woman and an unknown white man in February 1818 on the coast of Maryland. He saw his mother only a handful of times before her death when he was seven. Frederick knew what it meant to suffer because he experienced firsthand the horrors of slavery, including continual whippings and lack of food.

However, Frederick's passion to be free was relentless. After being imprisoned for one failed escape attempt, he impersonated a sailor and traveled by train and steamboat to New York City. He didn't stay long in New York, moving on to New Bedford, Massachusetts, where he married Anna Murray and assumed the name Frederick Douglass.

Joining a black church there, he attended abolitionist meetings and discovered a talent for public speaking. His compelling message drew eager crowds. Despite fears of being recaptured, Douglass published three autobiographies, including *My Bondage and My Freedom*.

There's no way to overstate Douglass's contributions to the abolitionist movement. He not only met with Abraham Lincoln several times during the Civil War, but he also helped recruit African Americans from the North for the Union Army. And after the war, he continued to defend their rights and the rights of women.

In the following excerpt from *My Bondage and My Freedom*, Douglass tells of his first encounter with abolition and God. He describes the impact a white Methodist minister named Hanson, a man named Charles Johnson, and his uncle Lawson made on his spiritual journey. His story rings of a sense of destiny, a calling to something greater than himself—a calling that from every account he fulfilled. There's a sense of awe, wonder, and humility that God used a child born into slavery—with little to no knowledge of his mother or father—to do so much for so many. May Douglass's story be a source of inspiration to us all.

*Margaret*

FREDERICK DOUGLASS
Excerpted from *My Bondage and My Freedom* [14]

## CHAPTER XII: RELIGIOUS NATURE AWAKENED

I was all ears, all eyes, whenever the words *slave, slavery,* dropped from the lips of any white person, and the occasions were not unfrequent when these words became leading ones, in high, social debate, at our house, every little while, I could hear Master Hugh, or some of his company, speaking with much warmth and excitement about *"abolitionists."* Of *who* or *what* these were, I was totally ignorant. I found, however, that whatever they might be, they were most cordially hated and soundly abused by slaveholders, of every grade. I very soon discovered, too, that slavery was, in some sort, under consideration, whenever the abolitionists were alluded to.

This made the term a very interesting one to me. If a slave, for instance, had made good his escape from slavery, it was generally alleged, that he had been persuaded and assisted by the abolitionists. If, also, a slave killed his master—as was sometimes the case—or struck down his overseer, or set fire to his master's dwelling, or committed any violence or crime, out of the common way, it was certain to be said, that such a crime was the legitimate fruits of the abolition movement.

> To read Douglass's own story of his awakening to the abolitionist—or anti-slavery—movement is truly witnessing history in the making.

### Discovering Others Who Opposed Slavery

Hearing such charges often repeated, I, naturally enough, received the impression that abolition—whatever else it might be—could not be unfriendly to the slave, nor very friendly to the slaveholder. I therefore set about finding out, if possible, *who* and *what* the abolitionists were, and *why* they were so obnoxious to the slaveholders. The dictionary afforded me very little help. It taught me that abolition was the "act of abolishing;" but it left me in ignorance at the very point where I most wanted information—and that was, as to the *thing* to be abolished. A city newspaper, the "Baltimore American," gave me the incendiary information denied me by the dictionary. In its columns I found, that, on a certain day, a vast number of petitions and memorials had been presented to congress, praying for the abolition of slavery in the District of Columbia, and for the abolition of the slave trade between the states of the Union. This was enough. The vindictive bitterness, the marked caution, the studied reserve, and the cumbrous ambiguity, practiced by our white folks, when alluding to this subject, was now fully explained.

Ever, after that, when I heard the words "abolition," or "abolition movement," mentioned, I felt the matter one of a personal concern; and I drew near to listen, when I could do so, without seeming too solicitous and prying. There was Hope in those words. Ever and anon, too, I could see some terrible denunciation of slavery, in our papers—copied from abolition papers at the north,—and the injustice of such denunciation commented on.

These I read with avidity. I had a deep satisfaction in the thought, that the rascality of slaveholders was not concealed from the eyes of the world, and that I was not alone in abhorring the cruelty and brutality of slavery. . . .

> Consider for a moment what it must have been like to be a slave and discover what the word *abolition* meant. For Douglass, discovering that others believed what he did—that slavery was wrong—must have infused him with new life and courage.

### Discovering God

Previous to my contemplation of the anti-slavery movement, and its probable results, my mind had been seriously awakened to the subject of religion. I was not more than thirteen years old, when I felt the need of God, as a father and protector. My religious nature was awakened by the preaching of a white Methodist minister, named Hanson. He thought that all men, great and small, bond and free, were sinners in the sight of God; that they were, by nature, rebels against His government; and that they must repent of their sins, and be reconciled to God, through Christ. I cannot say that I had a very distinct notion of what was required of me; but one thing I knew very well—I was wretched, and had no means of making myself otherwise. Moreover, I knew that I could pray for light. I consulted a good colored man, named Charles Johnson; and, in tones of holy affection, he told me to pray, and what to pray for. I was, for weeks, a poor, broken-hearted mourner, traveling through the darkness and misery of doubts and fears. I finally found that change of heart which comes by "casting all one's care" upon God, and by having faith in Jesus Christ, as the Redeemer, Friend, and Savior of those who diligently seek Him.

*This is a profound spiritual moment of transformation in Douglass's life. It's a colorful, life-filled description of his discovery of God.*

After this, I saw the world in a new light. I seemed to live in a new world, surrounded by new objects, and to be animated by new hopes and desires. I loved all mankind—slaveholders not excepted; though I abhorred slavery more than ever. My great concern was, now, to have the world converted. The desire for knowledge increased, and especially did I want a thorough acquaintance with the contents of the bible. I have gathered scattered pages from this holy book, from the filthy street gutters of Baltimore, and washed and dried them, that in the moments of my leisure, I might get a word or two of wisdom from them. While thus religiously seeking knowledge, I became acquainted with a good old colored man, named Lawson. A more devout man than he, I never saw. He drove a dray for Mr. James Ramsey, the owner of a rope-walk on Fell's Point, Baltimore. This man not only prayed three times a day, but he prayed as he walked through the streets, at his work—on his dray—everywhere. His life was a life of prayer, and his words (when he spoke to his friends,) were about a better world. Uncle Lawson lived near Master Hugh's house; and, becoming deeply attached to the old man, I went often with him to prayer-meeting, and spent much of my leisure time with him on Sunday. The old man could read a little, and I was a great help to him, in making out the hard words, for I was a better reader than he.

God seemed to bring people like Uncle Lawson into Douglass's life to help him not only grow spiritually but also learn to write from the heart.

### Learning to Read and Write

I could teach him *"the letter,"* but he could teach me *"the spirit;"* and high, refreshing times we had together, in singing, praying and glorifying God. These meetings with Uncle Lawson went on for a long time, without the knowledge of Master Hugh or my mistress. Both knew, however, that I had become religious, and they seemed to respect my conscientious piety. My mistress was still a professor of religion, and belonged to class. Her leader was no less a person than the Rev. Beverly Waugh, the presiding elder, and now one of the bishops of the Methodist Episcopal church. Mr. Waugh was then stationed over Wilk street church. I am careful to state these facts, that the reader may be able to form an idea of the precise influences which had to do with shaping and directing my mind.

In view of the cares and anxieties incident to the life she was then leading, and, especially, in view of the separation from religious associations to which she was subjected, my mistress had, as I have before stated, become lukewarm, and needed to be looked up by her leader. This brought Mr. Waugh to our house, and gave me an opportunity to hear him exhort and pray. But my chief instructor, in matters of religion, was Uncle Lawson. He was my spiritual father; and I loved him intensely, and was at his house every chance I got.

Throughout Douglass's difficult early years, God was at work, even providing him with a spiritual mentor and the strength to remain steady through huge opposition.

This pleasure was not long allowed me. Master Hugh became averse to my going to Father Lawson's, and threatened to whip me if I ever went there again. I now felt myself persecuted by a wicked man; and I *would* go to Father Lawson's, notwithstanding the threat. The good old man had told me, that the "Lord had a great work for me to do;" and I must prepare to do it; and that he had been shown that I must preach the gospel. His words made a deep impression on my mind, and I verily felt that some such work was before me, though I could not see *how* I should ever engage in its performance. "The good Lord," he said, "would bring it to pass in his own good time," and that I must go on reading and studying the scriptures.

The advice and the suggestions of Uncle Lawson, were not without their influence upon my character and destiny. He threw my thoughts into a channel from which they have never entirely diverged. He fanned my already intense love of knowledge into a flame, by assuring me that I was to be a useful man in the world. When I would say to him, "How can these things be and what can *I* do?" his simple reply was, *"Trust in the Lord."* When I told him that *"I was a slave, and a slave FOR LIFE,"* he said, "the Lord can make you free, my dear. All things are possible with him, only *have faith in God." "Ask, and it shall be given." "*If you want liberty," said the good old man, "ask the Lord for it, *in faith*, AND HE WILL GIVE IT TO YOU. "

Thus assured, and cheered on, under the inspiration of hope, I worked and prayed with a light heart, believing that my life was under the guidance of a wisdom higher than my own. With all other blessings sought at the mercy seat, I always prayed that God would, of His great mercy, and in His own good time, deliver me from my bondage. . . .

After this manner I began to learn to write: I was much in the ship yard—Master Hugh's, and that of Durgan & Bailey—and I observed that the carpenters, after hewing and getting a piece of timber ready for use, wrote on it the initials of the name of that part of the ship for which it was intended. When, for instance, a piece of timber was

It's fascinating that God didn't only answer Douglass's prayer for freedom, but he used Douglass to help set countless others free as well.

ready for the starboard side, it was marked with a capital "S." A piece for the larboard side was marked "L;" larboard forward, "L. F.;" larboard aft, was marked "L. A.;" starboard aft, "S. A.;" and starboard forward "S. F." I soon learned these letters, and for what they were placed on the timbers.

My work was now, to keep fire under the steam box, and to watch the ship yard while the carpenters had gone to dinner. This interval gave me a fine opportunity for copying the letters named. I soon astonished myself with the ease with which I made the letters; and the thought was soon present, "if I can make four, I can make more." But having made these easily, when I met boys about Bethel church, or any of our play-grounds, I entered the lists with them in the art of writing, and would make the letters which I had been so fortunate as to learn, and ask them to "beat that if they could." With play-mates for my teachers, fences and pavements for my copy books, and chalk for my pen and ink, I learned the art of writing. I, however, afterward adopted various methods of improving my hand. The most successful, was copying the *italics* in Webster's spelling book, until I could make them all without looking on the book. By this time, my little "Master Tommy" had grown to be a big boy, and had written over a number of copy books, and brought them home. They had been shown to the neighbors, had elicited due praise, and were now laid carefully away. Spending my time between the ship yard and house, I was as often the lone keeper of the latter as of the former. When my mistress left me in charge of the house, I had a grand time; I got Master Tommy's copy books and a pen and ink, and, in the ample spaces between the lines, I wrote other lines, as nearly like his as possible. The process was a tedious one, and I ran the risk of getting a flogging for marring the highly prized copy books of the oldest son.

In addition to those opportunities, sleeping, as I did, in the kitchen loft—a room seldom visited by any of the family,—I got a flour barrel up

In a very shrewd way, Douglass teaches himself to write. He not only learns from children, but he also is willing to hand copy everything, from the dictionary to the Bible to hymns—just to become literate.

there, and a chair; and upon the head of that barrel I have written (or endeavored to write,) copying from the bible and the Methodist hymn book, and other books which had accumulated on my hands, till late at night, and when all the family were in bed and asleep. I was supported in my endeavors by renewed advice, and by holy promises from the good Father Lawson, with whom I continued to meet, and pray, and read the scriptures. Although Master Hugh was aware of my going there, I must say, for his credit, that he never executed his threat to whip me, for having thus, innocently, employed my leisure time.

Douglass's story continues beyond this point. He became one of the nation's greatest speakers and continued an uphill battle for civil rights for the next several decades. His life is an example of what God can do through a person of passion and courage.

# VITAL STATS

**WHEN AND WHERE:** Andrew Murray was born in South Africa and ended up studying in Scotland and Holland. After finishing his studies, he returned to South Africa.

**STYLE:** Andrew Murray passionately loved truth and discovered the importance of a vibrant prayer life. He loved telling stories about the good news of the gospel.

**NOTEWORTHY ACCOMPLISHMENT:** He wrote over two hundred books, mostly on prayer. His book *Absolute Surrender* is perhaps one of his most memorable.

**TIMELESS WISDOM:** Andrew Murray's life is a reminder still today that God is willing to work in us to help us surrender fully to him. He provides all the strength we need; we just have to stay close to him.

Ever have trouble knowing how to talk with God? After all, how do you communicate with someone you can't see? Depending on your spiritual background, you may know a lot or very little about what it means to *abide* in Christ, to really experience the depths of a relationship with him. And what about the whole idea of surrendering your life to him? *That* can be truly intimidating—even threatening—to anyone who hasn't quite grasped the joys of giving over control of their life to God's loving plans.

Well, I'd like to introduce you to someone who really got all those concepts: prayer, abiding in Christ, and surrendering everything to him. Meet Andrew Murray, one of history's most influential preachers and writers of the nineteenth century.

Born in 1828 in Graaff Reinet, South Africa, to a preacher and his wife, Andrew Murray learned at an early age the value of putting God first in his life. Growing up in the Murray home meant being raised in a lifestyle of consistent prayer, conservative biblical teaching, and grace-filled worship.

**ANDREW MURRAY 1828–1917**

One of Murray's passions as a youngster was watching his dad minister, bringing the Good News of Jesus Christ to the Dutch settlers of South Africa; in fact, it was his longing to one day follow in his father's footsteps and do the Lord's work with the Dutchmen. At age ten, a mature-beyond-his-years Murray was sent away to Scotland for schooling. He finished high school, went to college, and then moved to Holland to study theology and pastoral ministry.

At the very young age of twenty, Murray became an ordained minister. Upon finishing his seminary work, he returned to South Africa and, true to his early plans, joined his father in ministering to the Dutch settlers.

I was introduced to Murray's career through a dear preacher friend of mine who studied at a prestigious London seminary. My friend had become familiar with Murray's written works through a class there. Some of Murray's books were a powerful influence on how he eventually began to view the gifts of the Spirit, pure love, and faith. During his time in London, my friend would e-mail me from time to time with excerpts of his favorite Murray sermons and writings. Murray's words were a great encouragement to me, too.

My friend encouraged me to get Murray's book *Absolute Surrender*. Because it's now out of print, it took me almost a year before I could even find it used. But it was worth the wait. It would be an understatement to suggest that the book is anything less than an inspirational glance at godly truth—a glance that has greatly influenced the way I think about Jesus.

Andrew Murray's sincere understanding and study of Scripture led him to write many books and devotionals. The following chapter, "The Fruit of the Spirit Is Love," is one of my favorites from *Absolute Surrender*. I believe Murray's words will challenge and inspire you to a deeper understanding of what it means to love. And if you can find a copy of the book, I highly recommend giving it a chance—it will impact the way you think about your spiritual future.

*Matthew*

## ANDREW MURRAY
Excerpted from *Absolute Surrender*[15]

### THE FRUIT OF THE SPIRIT IS LOVE

I want to look at the fact of a life filled with the Holy Spirit more from the practical side, and to show how this life will show itself in our daily walk and conduct.

Under the Old Testament you know the Holy Spirit often came upon men as a divine Spirit of revelation to reveal the mysteries of God, or for power to do the work of God. But He did not then dwell in them. Now, many just want the Old Testament gift of power for work, but know very little of the New Testament gift of the indwelling Spirit, animating and renewing the whole life. When God gives the Holy Spirit, His great object is the formation of a holy character. It is a gift of a holy mind and spiritual disposition, and what we need above everything else, is to say:

"I must have the Holy Spirit sanctifying my whole inner life if I am really to live for God's glory." You might say that when Christ promised the Spirit to the disciples, He did so that they might have power to be witnesses. True, but then they received the Holy Ghost in such heavenly power and reality that He took possession of their whole being at once and so fitted them as holy men for doing the work with power as they had to do it. Christ spoke of power to the disciples, but it was the Spirit filling their whole being that worked the power.

I wish now to dwell upon the passage found in Galatians 5:22: "The fruit of the Spirit is love."

We read that "Love is the fulfilling of the law," and my desire is to speak on love as a fruit of the Spirit with a twofold object. One is that this word may be a searchlight in our hearts, and give us a test by which to try all our thoughts about the Holy Spirit and all our experience of the holy life. Let us try ourselves by this word. Has this been our daily habit, to seek the being filled with the Holy Spirit as the Spirit of love? "The fruit of the Spirit is

Right up front,
Murray issues a time-
less challenge for
the reader: Is the
Holy Spirit's work
obvious in your life?

love." Has it been our experience that the more we have of the Holy Spirit the more loving we become? In claiming the Holy Spirit we should make this the first object of our expectation. The Holy Spirit comes as a Spirit of love.

Oh, if this were true in the Church of Christ how different her state would be! May God help us to get hold of this simple, heavenly truth that the fruit of the Spirit is a love which appears in the life, and that just as the Holy Spirit gets real possession of the life, the heart will be filled with real, divine, universal love.

One of the great causes why God cannot bless His Church is *the want of love*. When the body is divided, there cannot be strength. In the time of their great religious wars, when Holland stood out so nobly against Spain, one of their mottoes was: "Unity gives strength." It is only when God's people stand as one body, one before God in the fellowship of love, one toward another in deep affection, one before the world in a love that the world can see—it is only then that they will have power to secure the blessing which they ask of God. Remember that if a vessel that ought to be one whole is cracked into many pieces, it cannot be filled. You can take a potsherd, one part of a vessel, and dip out a little water into that, but if you want the vessel full, the vessel must be whole. That is literally true of Christ's Church, and if there is one thing we must pray for still, it is this: Lord, melt us together into one by the power of the Holy Spirit; let the Holy Spirit, who at Pentecost made them all of one heart and one soul, do His blessed work among us. Praise God, we can love each other in a divine love, for "the fruit of the Spirit is love." Give yourselves up to love, and the Holy Spirit will come; receive the Spirit, and He will teach you to love more.

## GOD IS LOVE

Now, why is it that the fruit of the Spirit is love? *Because God is love.*

And what does that mean?

It is the very nature and being of God to delight in communicating

Himself. God has no selfishness, God keeps nothing to Himself. God's nature is to be always giving. In the sun and the moon and the stars, in every flower you see it, in every bird in the air, in every fish in the sea. God communicates life to His creatures. And the angels around His throne, the seraphim and cherubim who are flames of fire — whence have they their glory? It is because God is love, and He imparts to them of His brightness and His blessedness. And we, His redeemed children — God delights to pour His love into us. And why? Because, as I said, God keeps nothing for Himself. From eternity God had His only begotten Son, and the Father gave Him all things, and nothing that God had was kept back. "God is love."

One of the old Church fathers said that we cannot better understand the Trinity than as a revelation of divine love — the Father, the loving One, the Fountain of love; the Son, the beloved one, the Reservoir of love, in whom the love was poured out; and the Spirit, the living love that united both and then overflowed into this world.

> With simple eloquence, Murray describes the overflow of God's generous love to the world as a whole, as well as individual lives.

The Spirit of Pentecost, the Spirit of the Father, and the Spirit of the Son is love. And when the Holy Spirit comes to us and to other men, will He be less a Spirit of love than He is in God? It cannot be; He cannot change His nature. The Spirit of God is love, and "the fruit of the Spirit is love."

## MANKIND NEEDS LOVE

Why is that so? That was the one great need of mankind, that was the thing which Christ's redemption came to accomplish: *to restore love to this world.*

When man sinned, why was it that he sinned? Selfishness triumphed — he sought self instead of God. And just look! Adam at once begins to accuse the woman of having led him astray. Love to God had gone, love to man was lost. Look again: of the first two children of Adam the one becomes a murderer of his brother.

Does not that teach us that sin had robbed the world of love? Ah! what a proof the history of the world has been of love having been lost! There may have been beautiful examples of love even among the heathen, but only as a little remnant of what was lost. One of the worst things sin did for man was to make him selfish, for selfishness cannot love.

The Lord Jesus Christ came down from Heaven as the Son of God's love. "God so loved the world that He gave His only begotten Son." God's Son came to show what love is, and He lived a life of love here upon earth in fellowship with His disciples, in compassion over the poor and miserable, in love even to His enemies, and He died the death of love. And when He went to Heaven, whom did He send down? The Spirit of love, to come and banish selfishness and envy and pride, and bring the love of God into the hearts of men. "The fruit of the Spirit is love."

And what was the preparation for the promise of the Holy Spirit? You know that promise as found in the fourteenth chapter of John's Gospel. But remember what precedes in the thirteenth chapter. Before Christ promised the Holy Spirit, He gave a new commandment, and about that new commandment He said wonderful things. One thing was: "Even as I have loved you, so love ye one another." To them His dying love was to be the only law of their conduct and intercourse with each other. What a message to those fishermen, to those men full of pride and selfishness! "Learn to love each other," said Christ, "as I have loved you." And by the grace of God they did it. When Pentecost came, they were of one heart and one soul. Christ did it for them.

> Jesus came to show us how to love. When he returned to heaven, he sent his Holy Spirit to continue the work of helping us learn to love as he does. If the world would truly get that, what a different place it'd be!

And now He calls us to dwell and to walk in love. He demands that though a man hate you, still you love him. True love cannot be conquered by anything in Heaven or upon the earth. The more hatred there is, the more love triumphs through it all and shows its true nature. This is the love that Christ commanded His disciples to exercise.

What more did He say? "By this shall all men know that ye are my disciples, if ye have love one to another."

You all know what it is to wear a badge. And Christ said to His disciples in effect: "I give you a badge, and that badge is love. That is to be your mark. It is the only thing in Heaven or on earth by which men can know me." Do we not begin to fear that love has fled from the earth? That if we were to ask the world: "Have you seen us wear the badge of love?" the world would say: "No; what we have heard of the Church of Christ is that there is not a place where there is no quarreling and separation." Let us ask God with one heart that we may wear the badge of Jesus' love. God is able to give it.

## LOVE CONQUERS SELFISHNESS

"The fruit of the Spirit is love." Why? *Because nothing but love can expel and conquer our selfishness.*

Self is the great curse, whether in its relation to God, or to our fellow-men in general, or to fellow-Christians, thinking of ourselves and seeking our own. Self is our greatest curse. But, praise God, Christ came to redeem us from self. We sometimes talk about deliverance from the self-life — and thank God for every word that can be said about it to help us — but I am afraid some people think deliverance from the self-life means that now they are going to have no longer any trouble in serving God; and they forget that deliverance from self-life means to be a vessel overflowing with love to everybody all the day.

And there you have the reason why many people pray for the power of the Holy Ghost, and they get something, but oh, so little! because they prayed for power for work, and power for blessing, but they have not prayed for power for full deliverance from self. That means not only the righteous self in intercourse with God, but also the unloving self in intercourse with men. And there is deliverance. "The fruit of the Spirit is love." I bring you the glorious promise of Christ that He is able to fill our hearts with love.

*Murray goes deeper in his discussion of the destructive power of selfishness and the healing strength of love.*

A great many of us try hard at times to love. We try to force ourselves to love, and I do not say that is wrong; it is better than nothing. But the end of it is always very sad. "I fail continually," such as one must confess. And what is the reason? The reason is simply this: Because they have never learned to believe and accept the truth that the Holy Spirit can pour God's love into their heart. That blessed text; often it has been limited! — "The love of God is shed abroad in our hearts." It has often been understood in this sense: It means the love of God to me. Oh, what a limitation! That is only the beginning. The love of God is always the love of God in its entirety, in its fullness as an indwelling power, a love of God to me that leaps back to Him in love, and overflows to my fellow-men in love—God's love to me, and my love to God, and my love to my fellowmen. The three are one; you cannot separate them. Do believe that the love of God can be shed abroad in your heart and mine so that we can love all the day. . . .

And how can I learn to love? Never until the Spirit of God fills my heart with God's love, and I begin to long for God's love in a very different sense from which I have sought it so selfishly, as a comfort and a joy and a happiness and a pleasure to myself; never until I begin to learn that "God is love," and to claim it, and receive it as an indwelling power for self-sacrifice; never until I begin to see that my glory, my blessedness, is to be like God and like Christ, in giving up everything in myself for my fellowmen. May God teach us that! Oh, the divine blessedness of the love with which the Holy Spirit can fill our hearts! "The fruit of the Spirit is love."

Murray uses inspiring (and convicting!) words about love guiding our daily living.

## LOVE IS GOD'S GIFT

Once again I ask, Why must this be so? And my answer is: *Without this we cannot live the daily life of love.*

How often, when we speak about the consecrated life, we have to speak about *temper*, and some people have sometimes said:

"You make too much of temper."

I do not think we can make too much of it. Think for a moment of a clock and of what its hands mean. The hands tell me what is within the clock, and if I see that the hands stand still, or that the hands point wrong, or that the clock is slow or fast, I say that something inside the clock is not working properly. And temper is just like the revelation that the clock gives of what is within. Temper is a proof whether the love of Christ is filling the heart, or not. . . .

Then there is the *tongue*! We sometimes speak of the tongue when we talk of the better life, and the restful life, but just think what liberty many Christians give to their tongues. They say:

"I have a right to think what I like."

When they speak about each other, when they speak about their neighbors, when they speak about other Christians, how often there are sharp remarks! God keep me from saying anything that would be unloving; God shut my mouth if I am not to speak in tender love. . . . Have you aimed at that? Have you sought it? Have you ever pleaded for it? Jesus Christ said: "As I have loved you . . . love one another." And He did not put that among the other commandments, but He said in effect:

"That is a new commandment, the one commandment: Love one another as I have loved you."

It is in our daily life and conduct that the fruit of the Spirit is love. From that there comes all the graces and virtues in which love is manifested: joy, peace, longsuffering, gentleness, goodness; no sharpness or hardness in your tone, no unkindness or selfishness; meekness before God and man. . . . The fruit of the Spirit that He brought from Heaven out of the heart of the crucified Christ, and that He gives in our heart, is first and foremost — love. . . .

Let a man be what he will, you are to love him. Love is to be the fruit of the Spirit all the day and every day. Yes, listen! if a man loves not his brother whom he hath seen — if you don't love that unlovable man whom you have seen, how can you love God whom you have not seen? You can deceive yourself with beautiful thoughts about loving God. You must prove your love to God by your love to your brother; that is the one standard by which God will judge your love to Him. If the love of God is in your heart you will love your brother. The fruit of the Spirit is love. . . .

## OUR LOVE SHOWS GOD'S POWER

Why are we taught that "the fruit of the Spirit is love"? *Because the Spirit of God has come to make our daily life an exhibition of divine power and a revelation of what God can do for His children.* . . .

Think of the church at large. What divisions! . . . That there are differences of opinion does not trouble me. We do not have the same constitution and temperament and mind. But how often hate, bitterness, contempt, separation, unlovingness are caused by the holiest truths of God's Word! Our doctrines, our creeds, have been more important than love. We often think we are valiant for the truth and we forget God's command to speak the truth *in love*. And it was so in the time of the Reformation between the Lutheran and Calvinistic churches. What bitterness there was [then] in regard to the Holy Supper, which was meant to be the bond of union among all believers! And so, down the ages, the very dearest truths of God have become mountains that have separated us.

If we want to pray in power, and if we want to expect the Holy Spirit to come down in power, and if we want indeed that God shall pour out His Spirit, we must enter into a covenant with God that we love one another with a heavenly love. Are you ready for that? Only that is true love that is large enough to take in all God's children, the most unloving and unlovable, and unworthy, and unbearable, and trying. If my vow — absolute surrender to God — was true, then it must mean absolute surrender to the divine love to fill me; to be a servant of love to love every child of God around me. "The fruit of the Spirit is love."

Oh, God did something wonderful when He gave Christ, at His right hand, the Holy Spirit to come down out of the heart of the Father and His everlasting love. And how we have degraded the Holy Spirit into a mere power by which we have to do our work! God forgive us! Oh, that the Holy Spirit might be held in honor as a power to fill us with the very life and nature of God and of Christ!

# VITAL STATS

**WHEN AND WHERE:** Quakers Hannah Whitall and her husband, Robert Pearsall Smith, were popular evangelists in America and England during the Holiness Movement of the late nineteenth century (a movement that taught of "Christian perfection" on earth). She was also active in the Women's Suffrage and Temperance movements.

**STYLE:** Hannah Whitall Smith was very popular because she didn't use excess amounts of emotional appeal or dramatic rhetoric in her speeches like most other women did in those days. She is said to have been a very matter-of-fact, down-to-earth speaker with a quiet logic that was powerful.

**NOTEWORTHY ACCOMPLISHMENTS:** She is best known for her classics, *The Christian's Secret of a Happy Life* and *The God of All Comfort*. It's amazing that she could write such inspirational and uplifting works, considering she lost several children to different illnesses and endured marital struggles and scandals through the years. She writes about comfort and happiness from an intensely personal collection of experiences.

**TIMELESS WISDOM:** God is enough. Whether you're seeking comfort at your lowest point, facing loneliness and rejection, or parked anywhere else along the journey in a lifelong search for fulfillment, God is more than enough in every circumstance. He brings peace, stillness, joy, and purpose in every moment, if we will simply accept it.

Where do you go when your world falls apart? When no one hears the secret tears splash on the pillow after a hard day, an ugly argument, or a painful loss? From where on earth can comfort come when pride is wounded or hearts are broken? Hannah Whitall Smith has the answer.

Not surprisingly, she says it isn't found "on earth" at all. It isn't found by mindlessly inhaling "comfort food" at the Cracker Barrel or in an emergency summit with all your best and most compassionate buddies. It isn't even found in mind-altering substances or Dr. Phil. Instead, she contends that real comfort, *soul* comfort, is found in God alone.

Now that is a beautiful concept, isn't it? Looks great on paper, for sure. But what's great about this piece is that she is transparent and open enough to admit it's easier to talk about finding comfort in God alone than it is to live it. She shares some of the traps we fall into and how we can really experience the abiding comfort Christ offers. (Hint: We have to believe him, trust his goodness, and choose to accept his comfort.) Her honesty and practicality make this reading easily applicable to life.

Like so many of my peers, I had never really experienced an overwhelming need for a face-to-face encounter with the comfort-filled side of God before my twenties. It sounds crazy now, but I think my first major need of *soul* comfort was the first night at college, all alone on a campus full of strangers. I felt so un-comforted, so un-comfortable. And to think, I was nearly inconsolable when graduation-day good-byes had to be said. I arrived at the university crying because I was there, and left crying because I couldn't stay anymore! Odd how that happens, isn't it?

Something slowly changed in me, though, and I learned to appreciate friends while we're together and refrain from letting "see you later" paralyze me with grief. Or so I thought. Until I had to face my first "see you in heaven" instead of "see you later." And it wasn't just anybody, either. It was my top prayer warrior and number-one fan, my role model, one of my closest soul sisters. When my grandmother died, I found out just what an amazing God of all comfort he really is.

There was nothing especially tragic or horrific about my grandmother's death or my sorrow, except that it was *my* sorrow, an extremely personal sorrow. After all, everyone goes through peaks and valleys. And most of it is just a normal part of the dreaded growing-up process. But every once in a while, situations arise and completely broadside us without warning. Losing a loved one, grieving the loss of a relationship, missing home, saying good-bye to old friends and hello to new ones—this life stage of the twenties decade can be really non-comforting!

Hannah Whitall Smith certainly understood this. She spent most of her twenties plagued by doubt and uncertainty. Later she lost a five-year-old child and had another child choose to live in rebellion. Her marriage to a popular nineteenth-century evangelist was shaky because of his reported immoral behavior. If anyone would know whether or not God offers comfort, she would! And she says he offers it freely, not only for some, but for *all*. And not only in some circumstances, but in *all*. He is the God of all comfort.

So next time your heart aches and your soul is weary, when it's your turn to hurt and grieve, pick up this classic by Hannah Whitall Smith. Reconnect with the God of All Comfort, and he will be the abiding refuge and strength you need to find hope again.

*Janella*

# HANNAH WHITALL SMITH
Excerpted from *The God of All Comfort*[16]

## CHAPTER 3: THE GOD OF ALL COMFORT

> *"Blessed be God, even the Father of our Lord Jesus Christ, the Father*
> *of mercies and the God of all comfort; who comforteth us in all our*
> *tribulations, that we may be able to comfort them which are in any*
> *trouble, by the comfort wherewith we ourselves are comforted of*
> *God."* . . .

It is easy enough to say a great many beautiful things about God being the
God of all comfort; but unless we know what it is to be really and truly
comforted ourselves, we might as well talk to the winds. People must read
in our lives what they hear in our words, or all our preaching is worse than
useless. It would be well for us to ask ourselves what they are reading in us.
Is it comfort or discomfort that voices itself in our daily walk and life?

### What Is Comfort?

But at this point I may be asked what I mean by the comfort God gives. Is it
a sort of pious grace, that may perhaps fit us for Heaven, but that is somehow unfit to bear the brunt of our everyday life with its trials and its pains?
Or is it an honest and genuine comfort, as we understand comfort, that en-
folds life's trials and pains in an all embracing peace?

With all my heart I believe it is the latter.

Comfort, whether human or divine, is pure and simple comfort, and is
nothing else. We none of us care for pious phrases, we want realities; and
the reality of being comforted and comfortable seems to me almost more
delightful than any other thing in life. We all know what it is. When as little
children we have cuddled up into our mother's lap after a fall or a misfor-
tune, and have felt her dear arms around us, and her soft kisses on our hair,

we have had comfort. When, as grown-up people, after a hard day's work, we have put on our
slippers and seated ourselves by the fire, in an easy
chair with a book, we have had comfort. . . . We
cannot fail, therefore, to understand the meaning
of this name of God, the "God of all comfort."

Whitall Smith says
it's not the failure to
understand God's
comfort that plagues
us, but rather the
failure to believe it.

But alas, we have failed to believe it. It has
seemed to us too good to be true. The joy and de-
light of it, if it were really a fact, have been more than our poor suspicious
natures could take in. We may venture to hope sometimes that little scraps
of comfort may be vouchsafed to us; but we have run away frightened at the
thought of the "all comfort" that is ours in the salvation of the Lord Jesus
Christ.

And yet what more could He have said about it than He has said: "As one
whom his mother comforteth, so will I comfort you; and ye shall be comforted." Notice the as and so in this passage: "As one whom his mother
comforteth, so will I comfort you." It is real comforting that is meant here;
the sort of comforting that a child feels when it is "dandled on its mother's
knees, and borne on her sides"; and yet how many of us have really believed
that God's comforting is actually as tender and true as a mother's comforting, or even half or quarter so real. . . .

## Comfort for Everyone

If any troubled doubting heart, any heart that is fearing continually every
day some form or other of evil should read these lines, let me tell you again
in trumpet tones that this is just what the Lord Jesus Christ is for—to care
for and comfort all who mourn. "All," remember, every single one, even
you yourself, for it would not be "all" if you were left out. You may be so
cast down that you can hardly lift up your head, but the apostle tells us that
He is the "God that comforteth those that are cast down"; the comforting
of Christ. All who mourn, all who are cast down—I love to think of such a
mission of comfort in a world of mourning like ours; and I long to see every

cast down and sorrowing heart comforted with this comforting of God. And our Comforter is not far off in Heaven where we cannot find Him. He is close at hand. He abides with us. When Christ was going away from this earth, He told His disciples that He would not leave them comfortless, but would send "another Comforter" who would abide with them forever. This Comforter, He said, would teach them all things, and would bring all things to their remembrance. And then He declared, as though it were the necessary result of the coming of this divine Comforter: "Peace I leave with you, my peace I give unto you; not as the world giveth, give I unto you. Let not your heart [therefore] be troubled, neither let it be afraid." Oh, how can we, in the face of these tender and loving words, go about with troubled and frightened hearts.

"Comforter"—what a word of bliss, if we only could realize it. Let us repeat it over and over to ourselves, until its meaning sinks into the very depths of our being. And an "abiding" Comforter, too, not one who comes and goes, and is never on hand when most needed, but one who is always present, and always ready to give us "joy for mourning, and the garment of praise for the spirit of heaviness."

> The constant "abiding" presence of God is the source of true, deep, *soul* comfort.

The very words *abiding Comforter* are an amazing revelation. Try to comprehend them. If we can have a human comforter to stay with us for only a few days when we are in trouble, we think ourselves fortunate; but here is a divine Comforter who is always staying with us, and whose power to comfort is infinite. Never, never ought we for a single minute to be without comfort. . . .

## Accept God's Comfort

But you may ask how you are to get hold of this divine comfort. My answer is that you must take it. God's comfort is being continually and abundantly given, but unless you will accept it you cannot have it.

Divine comfort does not come to us in any mysterious or arbitrary way.

It comes as the result of a divine method. The indwelling Comforter "brings to our remembrance" comforting things concerning our Lord,
and, if we believe them, we are comforted by
them. A text is brought to our remembrance, perhaps, or the verse of a hymn, or some thought
concerning the love of Christ and His tender care
for us. If we receive the suggestion in simple faith,
we cannot help being comforted. But if we refuse to listen to the voice of
our Comforter, and insist instead on listening to the voice of discourage-
ment or despair, no comfort can by any possibility reach our souls.

*Attitude and choice have a lot to do with whether we are comforted or whether we turn bitter and live our lives as inconsolable victims.*

It is very possible for even a mother to lavish in vain all her stores of
motherly comfort on a weeping child. The child sits up stiff and sullen, and
"refuses to be comforted." All her comforting words fall on unbelieving
ears. For to be comforted by comforting words it is absolutely necessary for
us to believe these words. God has spoken "com-
forting words" enough, one would think, to comfort a whole universe, and yet we see all around us
unhappy Christians, and worried Christians, and
gloomy Christians, into whose comfortless hearts
not one of these comforting words seems to be allowed to enter. . . .

The apostle tells us that whatsoever things are
written in the Scriptures are for our learning, in
order that we "through patience and comfort of
the Scriptures may have hope." But if we are to be
comforted by the Scriptures, we must first believe
them. Nothing that God has said can possibly
comfort a person who does not believe it to be
really true. . . . Always and in everything comfort
must follow faith, and can never precede it.

In this matter of comfort it is exactly as it is in

*In order to be comforted by the Scriptures, as Whitall Smith suggests, we must first know what the Scriptures say. The Holy Spirit can comfort us by bringing verses to mind, but if we've never read them or memorized them or spent any time discovering them in his Word, they won't be in the library of our mind.*

every other experience in the religious life. God says, "Believe, and then you can feel." We say, "Feel, and then we can believe." God's order is not arbitrary, it exists in the very nature of things; and in all earthly matters we recognize this, and are never so foolish as to expect to feel we have anything until we first believe that it is in our possession. I could not possibly feel glad that I had a fortune in the bank, unless I knew that it was really there. But in spiritual things we reverse God's order (which is the order of nature as well), and refuse to believe that we possess anything until we first feel as if we had it.

Let me illustrate. We are, let us suppose, overwhelmed with cares and anxieties. It often happens in this world. To comfort us in these circumstances the Lord assures us that we need not be anxious about anything, but may commit all our cares to Him, for He careth for us. We are all familiar with the passages where He tells us to "behold the fowls of the air," and to "consider the lilies of the field" and assures us that we are of much more value than they, and that, if He cares for them, He will much more care for us. One would think there was comfort enough here for every care or sorrow all the wide world over. To have God assume our cares and our burdens, and carry them for us; the Almighty God, the Creator of Heaven and earth, who can control everything, and foresee everything, and consequently can manage everything in the very best possible way, to have Him declare that He will undertake for us; what could possibly be a greater comfort? And yet how few people are really comforted by it.

Life lesson: Choose to believe God instead of inward feelings. Get your beliefs right, and the feelings will subsequently align themselves accordingly.

Why is this? Simply and only because they do not believe it. They are waiting to have an inward feeling that His words are true, before they will believe them. They look upon them as beautiful things for Him to say, and they wish they could believe them, but they do not think they can be true in their own special case, unless they can have an inward feeling that they are; and if they should speak out honestly, they would confess that, since they have no such inward feeling, they do not believe His words apply to them; and as a consequence they do not in the least expect Him actually to care for their affairs at all. "Oh, if I could only feel it was all true," we say; and God says, "Oh, if you would only believe it is all true!"

It is pure and simple unbelief that is at the bottom of all our lack of comfort, and absolutely nothing else. God comforts us on every side, but we simply do not believe His words of comfort.

*This is a good example of how Whitall Smith values logic, truth, and beliefs over emotions and feelings. You can always trust the truth of Scripture, but you certainly can't automatically trust feelings and emotions!*

### Choose to Be Comforted

The remedy for this is plain. If we want to be comforted, we must make up our minds to believe every single solitary word of comfort God has ever spoken; and we must refuse utterly to listen to any words of discomfort spoken by our own hearts, or by our circumstances. We must set our faces like a flint to believe, under each and every sorrow and trial, in the divine Comforter, and to accept and rejoice in His all-embracing comfort. I say, "set our faces like a flint," because, when everything around us seems out of sorts, it is not always easy to believe God's words of comfort. We must put our wills into this matter of being comforted, just as we have to put our wills into all other matters in our spiritual life. We must choose to be comforted.

It may seem impossible, when things look all wrong and uncared for, to believe that God really can be caring for us as a mother cares for her children; and, although we know perfectly well that He says He does care for us in just this tender and loving way, yet we say, "Oh, if I could only believe that, of course I should be comforted." Now here is just where our wills must come in. We *must* believe it. We must say to ourselves, "God says it, and it is true, and I am going to believe it, no matter how it looks." And then we must never suffer ourselves to doubt or question it again.

# VITAL STATS

**WHEN AND WHERE:** C. H. Spurgeon was to nineteenth-century England what D. L. Moody was to America. Although Spurgeon never attended theological school, by the age of twenty-one he was the most popular preacher in London.

**STYLE:** C. H. Spurgeon was a man who lived life and performed ministry with flair and accent. His authentic style rang true to the man that God created him to be. He was direct, and in many cases he offended those who came to him for one-on-one advice.

**NOTEWORTHY ACCOMPLISHMENTS:** C. H. Spurgeon was not only a powerful speaker, but he was also a prolific writer. *The Treasury of David* is a commentary on the entire book of Psalms. He wrote and published it weekly for several years. He also wrote numerous tracts and books containing materials that are used to this day in sermon and Bible study preparation.

**TIMELESS WISDOM:** "Trials teach us what we are; they dig up the soil, and let us see what we are made of." C. H. Spurgeon spoke these words from personal experience, because his health was a roller coaster of ups and downs throughout his life. It's easy to resist the idea of embracing problems, but they are the catalyst for growth if we approach them that way.

Not many would argue against calling Charles Haddon Spurgeon England's greatest pastor-evangelist of the nineteenth century. Through Spurgeon, God built the largest evangelical church in the world at that time.

When he was only nineteen, Spurgeon became pastor of the New Park Street Chapel. Although only eighty people heard his first sermon, his congregation grew and eventually moved to the Metropolitan Tabernacle. By the time of his death thirty-seven years later, thousands were hearing him every week. He was not only a powerful communicator, but a strong leader as well.

**CHARLES H. SPURGEON** 1834–1892

But he was not always such a strong person.

In his younger years, he followed his father around the countryside as the elder Spurgeon preached in many different churches. One particular Sunday marked a turning point in Charles's life. That morning's bitter-cold temperature and deep snowdrifts caused him to pass up the usual trip with his father; instead, he opted for a church closer to home. God obviously meant for him to be there, because the visiting preacher at that church looked directly at Spurgeon and said, "Young man, you look miserable."

It was all too true. Spurgeon had been struggling for a long time with the idea of sin and how to find God's forgiveness. It was as if that sermon were meant for him. That day, Spurgeon said, it was as if the cloud was gone and the light of the sun revealed to him the clear path to salvation and an eternal relationship with God.

The topic of salvation was central to his preaching, teaching, writing, and leadership of other preachers who came to him for guidance; and it was one of the primary reasons the Metropolitan Tabernacle continued to grow throughout the nearly four decades of his ministry.

Spurgeon's life and ministry show us what it means to be a leader on God's team. Even today his writings inspire countless pastors to become everything they can be for God. And they can inspire the rest of us to choose whom we will live for and what our lives will be about.

The following excerpt from *All of Grace* can help you better understand just what God can do through you when you're wholeheartedly committed to him. What will your life tell others about salvation? A challenging question for all of us!

*Dave*

# CHARLES H. SPURGEON
Excerpted from *All of Grace*[17]

## FAITH—WHAT IS IT?

What is faith? *It is made up of three things—knowledge, belief, and trust.* *Knowledge* comes first. "How shall they believe in him of whom they have not heard?" I want to be informed of a fact before I can possibly believe it. "Faith cometh by hearing"; we must first hear, in order that we may know what is to be believed. "They that know thy name shall put their trust in thee." A measure of knowledge is essential to faith; hence the importance of getting knowledge. "Incline your ear, and come unto me; hear, and your soul shall live." . . .

Endeavour to know more and more of Christ Jesus. Endeavour especially to know the doctrine of the sacrifice of Christ; for the point upon which saving faith mainly fixes itself is this— "God was in Christ, reconciling the world unto himself, not imputing their trespasses unto them." Know that Jesus was "made a curse for us, as it is written, Cursed is every one that hangeth on a tree." Drink deep of the doctrine of the substitutionary work of Christ; for therein lies the sweetest possible comfort to the guilty sons of men, since the Lord "made him to be sin for us, that we might be made the righteousness of God in him." Faith begins with knowledge.

The mind goes on to *believe* that these things are true. The soul believes that God is, and that

How many of us haven't wondered at some point just what faith is? Spurgeon dives right into this vital backbone of the Christian life. His argument that faith begins with knowledge appeals to the intellect.

Faith may be blind because it involves believing even when we cannot see all the evidence; however, it should not be in blind ignorance that we choose to believe.

He hears the cries of sincere hearts; that the gospel is from God; that justifi-cation by faith is the grand truth which God hath revealed in these last days by His Spirit more clearly than before. Then the heart believes that Jesus is verily and in truth our God and Saviour, the Redeemer of men, the Prophet, Priest, and King of His people. All this is accepted as sure truth, not to be called in question. I pray that you may at once come to this. . . .

### Faith and Trust

So far you have made an advance toward faith; only one more ingredient is needed to complete it, which is *trust*. Commit yourself to the merciful God; rest your hope on the gracious gospel; trust your soul on the dying and liv-ing Saviour; wash away your sins in the atoning blood; accept His perfect righteousness, and all is well. Trust is the lifeblood of faith; there is no sav-ing faith without it. The Puritans were accustomed to explain faith by the word "recumbency." It meant leaning upon a thing. Lean with all your weight upon Christ. It would be a better illustration still if I said, fall at full length, and lie on the Rock of Ages. Cast yourself upon Jesus; rest in Him; commit yourself to Him. That done, you have exercised saving faith. Faith is not a blind thing; for faith begins with knowledge. It is not a speculative thing; for faith believes facts of which it is sure. It is not an unpractical, dreamy thing; for faith trusts, and stakes its destiny upon the truth of reve-lation. That is one way of describing what faith is. . . .

Faith also believes that Christ will do what He has promised; that since He has promised to cast out none that come to Him, it is certain that He will not cast *us* out if we come to Him. Faith believes that since Jesus said, "The water that I shall give him shall be in him a well of water springing up into everlasting life," it must be true; and if *we* get this living Water from Christ it will abide in *us*, and will well up within *us* in streams of holy life. Whatever Christ has promised to do He will do, and we must believe this, so as to look for pardon, justification, preservation, and eter-nal glory from His hands, according as He has promised them to believers in Him. . . .

## WHY ARE WE SAVED BY FAITH?

Why is faith selected as the channel of salvation? No doubt this inquiry is often made. "By grace are ye saved *through faith*," is assuredly the doctrine of Holy Scripture, and the ordinance of God; but why is it so? Why is faith selected rather than hope, or love, or patience?

It becomes us to be modest in answering such a question, for God's ways are not always to be understood; nor are we allowed presumptuously to question them. Humbly we would reply that, as far as we can tell, faith has been selected as the channel of grace, because *there is a natural adaptation* in faith to be used as the receiver. Suppose that I am about to give a poor man an alms: I put it into his hand—why? Well, it would hardly be fitting to put it into his ear, or to lay it upon his foot; the hand seems made on purpose to receive. So, in our mental frame, faith is created on purpose to be a receiver: it is the hand of the man, and there is a fitness in receiving grace by its means. . . .

Next, God selects faith as the channel of salvation because *it is a sure method, linking man with God*. When man confides in God, there is a point of union between them, and that union guarantees blessing. Faith saves us because it makes us cling to God, and so brings us into connection with Him. I have often used the following illustration, but I must repeat it, because I cannot think of a better. I am told that years ago a boat was upset above the falls of Niagara, and two men were being carried down the current, when persons on the shore managed to float a rope out to them, which rope was seized by them both. One of them held fast to it and was safely drawn to the bank; but the other, seeing a great log come floating by, unwisely let go the rope and clung to the log, for it was the bigger thing of the two, and apparently better to cling to. Alas! the log with the man on it went right over the vast abyss, because there was no union between the log and the shore. The size of the log was no benefit to him who grasped it; it needed a connection with the shore to produce safety. So when a man trusts to his works, or to sacraments, or to anything of that sort, he will not be saved, because there is no junction between him and Christ; but faith, though it may seem to be like a slender cord, is in the hands of the great God on the shore side; infinite power pulls in the connecting line, and thus draws the man from destruction. Oh the blessedness of faith, because it unites us to God!

Faith is the channel of grace because it is a sure method linking people with God.

Faith is chosen again, because *it touches the springs of action.* Even in common things faith of a certain sort lies at the root of all. I wonder whether I shall be wrong if I say that we never do anything except through faith of some sort. If I walk across my study it is because I believe my legs will carry me. A man eats because he believes in the necessity of food; he goes to business because he believes in the value of money; he accepts a check because he believes that the bank will honor it. . . . Most grand deeds have been born of faith; for good or for evil, faith works wonders by the man in whom it dwells. Faith in its natural form is an all-prevailing force, which enters into all manner of human actions. Possibly he who derides faith in God is the man who in an evil form has the most of faith; indeed, he usually falls into a credulity which would be ridiculous, if it were not disgraceful.

God gives salvation to faith, because by creating faith in us He thus touches the real mainspring of our emotions and actions. He has, so to speak, taken possession of the battery and now He can send the sacred current to every part of our nature. When we believe in Christ, and the heart has come into the possession of God, then we are saved from sin, and are moved toward repentance, holiness, zeal, prayer, consecration, and every other gracious thing. "What oil is to the wheels, what weights are to a clock, what wings are to a bird, what sails are to a ship, that faith is to all holy duties and services." Have faith, and all other graces will follow and continue to hold their course.

Faith, again, *has the power of working by love*; it influences the affections toward God, and draws the heart after the best things. He that believes in God will beyond all question love God. Faith is an act of the understanding; but it also proceeds from the heart. "With the heart man believeth unto righteousness"; and hence God gives salvation to faith because it resides next door to the affections, and is near akin to love; and love is the parent and the nurse of every holy feeling and act. Love to God is obedience, love to God is holiness. To love God and to love man is to be conformed to the image of Christ; and this is salvation.

Moreover, *faith creates peace and joy*; he that hath it rests, and is tranquil, is glad and joyous, and this is a preparation for heaven. God gives all heavenly gifts to faith, for this reason among others, that faith worketh in us the life and spirit which are to be eternally manifested in the upper and better world. Faith furnishes us with armor for this life, and education for the life to come. It enables a man both to live and to die without fear; it prepares both for action and for suffering; and hence the Lord selects it as a most convenient medium for conveying grace to us, and thereby securing us for glory.

Certainly faith does for us what nothing else can do; it gives us joy and peace, and causes us to enter into rest. Why do men attempt to gain salvation by other means? An old preacher says, "A silly servant who is bidden to open a door, sets his shoulder to it and pushes with all his might; but the door stirs not, and he cannot enter, use what strength he may. Another comes with a key, and easily unlocks the door, and enters right readily.

> Faith has the power of love, and it creates peace and joy. What more do we need? In that five-letter word lie the keys to a successful life.

Those who would be saved by works are pushing at heaven's gate without result; but faith is the key which opens the gate at once." Reader, will you not use that key? The Lord commands you to believe in His dear Son, therefore you may do so; and doing so you shall live. Is not this the promise of the gospel, "He that believeth and is baptized shall be saved"? (Mark 16:16). What can be your objection to a way of salvation which commends itself to the mercy and the wisdom of our gracious God?

# VITAL STATS

**WHEN AND WHERE:** D. L. Moody was born in New England and ministered throughout America, England, Scotland, and Ireland.

**STYLE:** He is well-known as a powerful preacher both in America and in Europe. When he preached, people showed up. It was not uncommon for crowds to top twelve to fifteen thousand at his evangelistic campaigns.

**NOTEWORTHY ACCOMPLISHMENTS:** The Sunday school D. L. Moody began in Chicago drew the attention of then-newly elected U.S. President Abraham Lincoln, who came and spoke at one of those meetings. Moody served as the president of the Chicago YMCA for three years following the Civil War. During his years as an evangelist, he began Chicago's Moody Bible Institute and Moody Church, both of which are still operating today.

**TIMELESS WISDOM:** D. L. Moody's life is proof that our beginnings are not limitations for God. He merely lived his passion for Christ and let God lead him. Just take a look at the results.

"The world has yet to see what God can do with, and for, and through, and in, and by, the man fully consecrated to Him."

These words from fellow evangelist Henry Varley ignited Dwight Lyman Moody's imagination and gave him a vision for living full tilt to the glory of God. In fact, Moody's life motto was "By God's help, I aim to be that man."

Moody's story is truly rare. A trendsetter, an encourager, a disciple-maker—he was all these things. But most of all he had a passion for helping others find the joy he knew in knowing Christ as Savior. He preached the gospel to more than one-hundred million people—without the help of TV or other modern media. His energy and vision brought to life ministry projects in both publishing and education.

Born on a small New England farm in 1837, Moody was the seventh of nine children. His father died when Dwight

**DWIGHT L. MOODY 1837–1899**

was only four years old, and his mother struggled to make ends meet and keep the family together.

At seventeen, he moved to Boston and got a job as a shoe salesman. But little did he know the turn his life would take one day when his Sunday school teacher walked into the store and led him to accept Christ as his Savior.

In 1860, with newfound direction and purpose, Moody traded his lucrative career for a life of full-time ministry. He moved to Chicago, and over the next several years he drew children to his flourishing Sunday school classes, which numbered up to 1,500 students.

Always eager to reach more people, Moody next set sail for England to expand the borders of his ministry and to learn from great European evangelists (such as Charles H. Spurgeon, incidentally). Before long, his name became well-known throughout America and Great Britain as he led thousands to Christ during numerous evangelistic campaigns. As he grew in his relationship with God, his preaching became even more effective. Some say he may have influenced nearly one million people with the message of salvation.

In addition to founding Moody Church and Moody Bible Institute, D. L. Moody also founded the Northfield schools in Massachusetts. And he served as the YMCA president for three years in his lifelong passion for getting the gospel message to youth. Undoubtedly, his own humble upbringing and meager formal education gave him a sensitivity for others in need. Despite the great demands on his time and energy, Moody always kept a high priority of investing in people; and throughout his enormous successes, his friends and colleagues attested to his truly humble nature.

In his book, *A Passion for Souls: The Life of D. L. Moody*, Lyle Dorsett offers ten reasons why Moody was so successful: (1) commitment, (2) willingness to take risks, (3) vision, (4) sensitivity to the Holy Spirit, (5) high view of Scripture, (6) Christ-centered life, (7) confidence in young people, (8) teachability, (9) love for souls, and (10) humility.[18]

The following excerpt is from "The Overcoming Life," a sermon Moody wrote in 1896. His words will encourage you to understand that *humility is not hesitation.* It is not being passive or seeking under-achievement. It is not becoming worthless or insignificant.

Humility is rather the compass that directs your purpose and the springboard that launches you into powerful service for God. May D. L. Moody's message spur you on toward a deeper understanding of God's work in your own story.

*Dave*

# DWIGHT L. MOODY
Excerpted from "The Overcoming Life" [19]

### The Tough Lesson of Humility

"Learn of me, for I am meek and lowly in heart" (Matthew 11:29).

There is no harder lesson to learn than the lesson of humility. It is not taught in the schools of men, only in the schools of Christ. It is the rarest of all gifts. Very rarely do we find a man or woman who is following closely the footsteps of the Master in meekness and in humility. I believe that it is the hardest lesson which Jesus Christ had to teach His disciples while He was here upon earth. It almost looked at first as though He had failed to teach it to the twelve men who had been with Him almost constantly for three years.

I believe that if we are humble enough we shall be sure to get a great blessing. After all, I think that more depends upon us than upon the Lord, because He is always ready to give a blessing and give it freely, but we are not always in a position to receive it. He always blesses the humble, and, if we can get down in the dust before Him, no one will go away disappointed. It was Mary at the feet of Jesus, who had chosen the "better part."

Did you ever notice the reason Christ gave for learning of Him? He might have said: "Learn of Me, because I am the most advanced thinker of the age. I have performed miracles that no man else had performed. I have shown My supernatural power in a thousand ways." But no: the reason He gave was that He was "meek, and lowly in heart."

We read of the three men in Scripture whose faces shone, and all three were noted for their meekness and humility. We are told that the face of Christ shone at His transfiguration; Moses, after he had been in the mount for forty days, came down from his communion with God with a shining face; and when Stephen stood before the Sanhedrin on the day of his death, his face was lighted up with glory. If our faces are to shine we must get into the valley of humility; we must go down in the dust before God. . . .

Some years ago I saw what is called a sensitive plant. I happened to breathe on it, and suddenly it drooped its head. I touched it, and it withered away. Humility is as sensitive as that; it cannot safely be brought out on exhibition. A man who is flattering himself that he is humble and is walking close to the Master, is self-deceived. It consists not in thinking meanly of ourselves, but in not thinking of ourselves at all. Moses [knew] not that his face shone. If humility speaks of itself, it is gone. . . .

A man can counterfeit love, he can counterfeit faith, he can counterfeit hope and all the other graces, but it is very difficult to counterfeit humility. You soon detect mock humility. They have a saying in the East among the Arabs, that as the tares and the wheat grow they show which God has blessed. The ears that God has blessed bow their heads and acknowledge every grain, and the more fruitful they are the lower their heads are bowed. The tares which God has sent as a curse, lift up their heads erect, high above the wheat, but they are only fruitful of evil. . . .

> Convicting words. It's not easy to deal with our own humility because our human nature wants recognition—even for being so humble!

### Humility in the Bible

As I have been studying some Bible characters that illustrate humility, I have been ashamed of myself. If you have any regard for me, pray that I may have humility. When I put my life beside the life of some of these men, I say, Shame on the Christianity of the present day. If you want to get a good idea of yourself, look at some of the Bible characters that have been clothed with meekness and humility, and see what a contrast is your position before God and man.

One of the meekest characters in history was John the Baptist. You remember when they sent a deputation to him and asked if he was Elias, or this prophet, or that prophet, and he said, "No." Now he might have said some very flattering things of himself. He might have said:

"I am the son of the old priest Zacharias. Haven't you heard of my fame as a preacher? I have baptized more people, probably, than any man living. The world has never seen a preacher like myself."

I honestly believe that in the present day most men standing in his position would do that. On the railroad train, some time ago, I heard a man talking so loud that all the people in the car could hear him. He said that he had baptized more people than any man in his denomination. He told how many thousand miles he had traveled, how many sermons he had preached, how many open-air services he had held, and this and that, until I was so ashamed that I had to hide my head. This is the age of boasting. It is the day of the great "I."

My attention was recently called to the fact that in all the Psalms you cannot find any place where David refers to his victory over the giant, Goliath. If it had been in the present day, there would have been a volume written about it at once; I don't know how many poems there would be telling of the great things that this man had done. He would have been in demand as a lecturer, and would have added a title to his name: G. G. K.,—Great Giant Killer. That is how it is today: great evangelists, great preachers, great theologians, great bishops. . . .

When his disciples came and told John that Christ was beginning to draw crowds, he nobly answered: "A man can receive nothing, except it be given him from heaven. [You] yourselves bear me witness that I said, I am not the Christ, but that I am sent before Him. He that hath the bride is the bridegroom: but the friend of the bridegroom, which standeth and heareth him, rejoiceth greatly because of the bridegroom's voice: this my joy therefore is fulfilled. He must increase, but I must decrease." . . .

Moody calls his day—over one hundred years ago—the age of boasting, the day of the great "I." Nothing's changed much in the past century. Consider how popular the phrase "It's not about me" has become recently.

### Humility Personalized

Let us now turn the light upon ourselves. Have we been decreasing of late? Do we think less of ourselves and of our position than we did a year ago? Are we seeking to obtain some position of dignity? Are we wanting to hold on to some title, and are we offended because we are not treated with the courtesy that we think is due us?

This is a powerful reminder to check our priorities. What are we pursuing— our own advancement or God's?

Some time ago I heard a man in the pulpit say that he should take offense if he was not addressed by his title. My dear friend, are you going to take that position that you must have a title, and that you must have every letter addressed with that title or you will be offended? John did not want any title, and when we are right with God, we shall not be caring about titles. In one of his early epistles Paul calls himself the "least of all of the apostles." Later on he claims to be "less than the least of all saints," and again, just before his death, humbly declares that he is the "chief of sinners." Notice how he seems to have grown smaller and smaller in his own estimation. So it was with John. And I do hope and pray that as the days go by we may feel like hiding ourselves, and let God have all the honor and glory. . . .

My dear friends, isn't it humiliating? Sometimes I think it is a wonder that any man is converted these days. Let another praise you. Don't be around praising yourself. If we want God to lift us up, let us get down. The lower we get, the higher God will lift us. It is Christ's eulogy of John, "Greater than any man born of woman." . . .

### Jesus, the King of Humility
The one prominent virtue of Christ, next to His obedience, is His humility; and even His obedience grew out of His humility. Being in the form of God, He counted it not a thing to be grasped to be on an equality with God, but He emptied Himself, taking the form of a bond-servant, and was made in the likeness of men. And being found in fashion as a man, He humbled Himself, and became obedient unto death, yea, the death of the cross. In His lowly birth, His submission to His earthly parents, His seclusion during thirty years, His consorting with the poor and despised, His entire submission and dependence upon His Father, this virtue that was consummated in His death on the cross, shines out.

One day Jesus was on His way to Capernaum and was talking about His coming death and suffering, and about His resurrection, and He heard quite a heated discussion going on behind Him. When he came into the house at Capernaum, He turned to His disciples and said,

"What was all that discussion about?"

I see John look at James, and Peter at Andrew,—and they all look ashamed. "Who shall be the greater?" That discussion has wrecked party after party, one society after another—"Who shall be the greatest?"

*Jesus' humble nature shined in everything he thought, said, and did. He calls us to follow his example.*

The way Christ took to teach them humility was by putting a little child in their midst and saying: "If you want to be great, take that little child for an example, and he who wants to be the greatest, let him be the servant of all."

To me, one of the saddest things in all the life of Jesus Christ was the fact that just before His crucifixion, His disciples should have been striving to see who should be the greatest, that night He instituted the Supper, and they ate the Passover together. It was His last night on earth, and they never saw Him so sorrowful before. He knew Judas was going to sell Him for thirty pieces of silver. He knew that Peter would deny Him. And yet, in addition to this, when going into the very shadow of the cross, there arose this strife as to who should be the greatest. He took a towel and girded Himself like a slave, and He took a basin of water and stooped and washed their feet.

That was another object lesson of humility. He said, "[You]call me Lord, and [you] do well. If you want to be great in my Kingdom, be servant of all. If you serve, you shall be great."

*Note Moody's point that it's the Holy Spirit's work in a person that develops humility. We can't accomplish it on our own.*

### The Humble Spirit at Work

When the Holy [Spirit] came, and those men were filled, from that time on mark the difference: Matthew takes up his pen to write, and he keeps Matthew out of sight. He tells what Peter and Andrew did, but he calls himself Matthew "the publican." He tells how they left all to follow Christ but does not mention the feast he gave. Jerome says that Mark's gospel is to be regarded as memoirs of Peter's discourses, and to have been published by his authority. Yet here we constantly find that damaging things are mentioned about Peter, and things to his credit are not referred to. Mark's gospel omits all allusion to Peter's faith in venturing on the sea, but goes into detail about the story of his fall and denial of our Lord. Peter put himself down, and lifted others up.

If the Gospel of Luke had been written to-day, it would be signed by the great Dr. Luke, and you would have his photograph as a frontispiece. But you can't find Luke's name; he keeps out of sight. He wrote two books, and his name is not to be found in either. John covers himself always under the expression—"the disciple whom Jesus loved." None of the four men whom history and tradition assert to be the authors of the gospels lay claim to the authorship in their writings. Dear man of God, I would that I had the same spirit, that I could just get out of sight,—hide myself.

My dear friends, I believe our only hope is to be filled with the Spirit of Christ. May God fill us, so that we shall be filled with meekness and humility. Let us take the hymn, "O, to be nothing, nothing," and make it the language of our hearts. It breathes the spirit of Him who said: "The Son can do *nothing* of himself!"

# VITAL STATS

**WHEN AND WHERE:** A London native, G. K. Chesterton was influential during World War I and the Great Depression.

**STYLE:** Known as a fun-loving and gregarious man, G. K. Chesterton was often noted for his quick wit and a contagious sense of humor. Despite his jolly frame, he struggled with thoughts of suicide as an adolescent, but he found answers to many of life's toughest questions in Christianity.

**NOTEWORTHY ACCOMPLISHMENTS:** His publishing accomplishments include more than one hundred books, five plays, five novels, hundreds of short stories and poems, as well as more than four thousand newspaper articles. Despite his strong opinions on a variety of religious and political issues, Chesterton was able to maintain warm, lifelong friendships with many of his biggest antagonists, including George Bernard Shaw, H. G. Wells, and J. M. Barrie.

**TIMELESS WISDOM:** "The Christian ideal has not been tried and found wanting; it has been found difficult and left untried," Chesterton observed. He spent much of his life defending the common man as well as the poor. In both his writings and speeches, he stood against the modern advances of atheism, materialism, and moral relativism long before they made their mighty imprint on the twenty-first century.

An old wooden closet, a witch on a sled, and some unusual talking animals invited me into the world of Narnia in C. S. Lewis's *The Lion, The Witch and the Wardrobe*. I couldn't resist the invitation. A group of lovable, renegade hobbits, a degenerated character named Gollum, and a desire to understand the power and mystery behind a golden ring welcomed me into the world of J. R. R. Tolkien's *The Lord of the Rings*. The journey was far longer and more dangerous than I ever anticipated. Lewis and Tolkien were only two of the great writers who transported me into their worlds so I could better understand my own.

Not all the adventures were quite as epic, at least in proportion.

Looking back, Dorothy's story was a short-lived adventure in the land of Oz. I still wonder why there weren't any sequels. Alice reminded me that everything in Wonderland deserves a second look. Charlie made my sugar fantasies come true in the chocolate factory. Anne of Green Gables taught me that anyone can change. James demonstrated that anything is possible as long as you have a giant peach. Mistress Mary reminded me of the importance of bravery when she explored the Secret Garden. And Peter Pan taught me that anyone, anywhere can learn to fly.

Through these and the other childhood friends I made through the books I read, I discovered the land of hobbits and elves and witches and the like. I learned of bravery and courage and sacrifice. I encountered worlds of mystery and wonder and power inconceivable. And along the way, I learned how to enter a world that couldn't be seen or smelled or touched. I learned the foundational lesson of faith.

In his groundbreaking book *Orthodoxy*, G. K. Chesterton includes the powerful essay, "The Ethics of Elfland," in which he invites us to reflect on the truths we once knew as children. In the process, he ushers a much-needed reminder about the importance of childlike faith.

In the following excerpts from this timeless essay, Chesterton suggests the existence of mystery and miracle in our world. While modern scientists hold a belief in the laws of nature, Chesterton suggests that there are other laws—laws of logic and reason—that govern the land. Fairy tales are willing to admit what the scientists are not—namely that there's a wonderful and miraculous nature all around us. The ability to be enchanted is not only an aspect of elfland but also a fundamental part of true Christianity.

Thus, our ability to *Oompah-Loompah, swallow a spoonful of sugar, follow the yellow brick road, and enter a world far different from the one we encounter every day may not be too far from orthodox faith.*

*Margaret*

# G. K. CHESTERTON
Excerpted from *Orthodoxy*[20]

## IV. THE ETHICS OF ELFLAND

### *Fed on Fairy Tales*

When the business man rebukes the idealism of his office-boy, it is commonly in some such speech as this: "Ah, yes, when one is young, one has these ideals in the abstract and these castles in the air; but in middle age they all break up like clouds, and one comes down to a belief in practical politics, to using the machinery one has and getting on with the world as it is."

Thus, at least, venerable and philanthropic old men now in their honoured graves used to talk to me when I was a boy. But since then I have grown up and have discovered that these philanthropic old men were telling lies. What has really happened is exactly the opposite of what they said would happen. They said that I should lose my ideals and begin to believe in the methods of practical politicians. Now, I have not lost my ideals in the least; my faith in fundamentals is exactly what it always was. What I have lost is my old childlike faith in practical politics. I am still as much concerned as ever about the Battle of Armageddon; but I am not so much concerned about the General Election. As a babe I leapt up on my mother's knee at the mere mention of it. No; the vision is always solid and reliable. The vision is always a fact. It is the reality that is often a fraud. As much as I ever did, more than I ever did, I believe in Liberalism. But there was a rosy time of innocence when I believed in Liberals. . . .

> Sometimes it seems like it's easier to make the leap of faith when you're young than when you're old.

My first and last philosophy, that which I believe in with unbroken certainty, I learnt in the nursery. I generally learnt it from a nurse; that is, from the solemn and star-appointed priestess at once of democracy and tradition. The things I believed most then, the things I believe most now, are the things called fairy tales. They seem to me to be the entirely reasonable things. They are not fantasies: compared with them other things are fantastic.

Compared with them religion and rationalism are both abnormal, though religion is abnormally right and rationalism abnormally wrong. Fairyland is nothing but the sunny country of common sense. It is not earth that judges heaven, but heaven that judges earth; so for me at least it was not earth that criticised elfland, but elfland that criticised the earth. I knew the magic beanstalk before I had tasted beans; I was sure of the Man in the Moon before I was certain of the moon. This was at one with all popular tradition. Modern minor poets are naturalists, and talk about the bush or the brook; but the singers of the old epics and fables were supernaturalists, and talked about the gods of brook and bush. That is what the moderns mean when they say that the ancients did not "appreciate Nature," because they said that Nature was divine. Old nurses do not tell children about the grass, but about the fairies that dance on the grass; and the old Greeks could not see the trees for the dryads.

But I deal here with what ethic and philosophy come from being fed on fairy tales. If I were describing them in detail I could note many noble and healthy principles that arise from them. There is the chivalrous lesson of "Jack the Giant Killer"; that giants should be killed because they are gigantic. It is a manly mutiny against pride as such. For the rebel is older than all the kingdoms, and the Jacobin has more tradition than the Jacobite. There is the lesson of "Cinderella," which is the same as that of the Magnificat— *exaltavit humiles*. There is the great lesson of "Beauty and the Beast"; that a thing must be loved *before* it is loveable. There is the terrible allegory of the "Sleeping Beauty," which tells how the human creature was blessed with all birthday gifts, yet cursed with death; and how death also may perhaps be softened to a sleep. But I am not concerned with any of the separate statutes of elfand, but with the whole spirit of its law, which I learnt before I could speak, and shall retain when I cannot write. I am concerned with a certain way of looking at life, which was created in me by the fairy tales, but has since been meekly ratified by the mere facts.

## A Reasonable Fairyland

It might be stated this way. There are certain sequences or developments (cases of one thing following another), which are, in the true sense of the word, reasonable. They are, in the true sense of the word, necessary. Such are mathematical and merely logical sequences. We in fairyland (who are the most reasonable of all creatures) admit that reason and that necessity. For instance, if the Ugly Sisters are older than Cinderella, it is (in an iron and awful sense) *necessary* that Cinderella is younger than the Ugly Sisters. There is no getting out of it. Haeckel may talk as much fatalism about that fact as he pleases: it really must be. If Jack is the son of a miller, a miller is the father of Jack. Cold reason decrees it from her awful throne: and we in fairyland submit.

If the three brothers all ride horses, there are six animals and eighteen legs involved: that is true rationalism, and fairyland is full of it. But as I put my head over the hedge of the elves and began to take notice of the natural world, I observed an extraordinary thing.

I observed that learned men in spectacles were talking of the actual things that happened—dawn and death and so on—as if *they* were rational and inevitable. They talked as if the fact that trees bear fruit were just as *necessary* as the fact that two and one trees make three. But it is not. There is an enormous difference by the test of fairyland; which is the test of the imagination. You cannot *imagine* two and one not making three. But you can easily imagine trees not growing fruit;

> If read too quickly, Chesterton's logical parallels can make your head spin! However, when given time to sink in, his points clearly support the idea that just because something is imaginative doesn't necessarily make it silly or useless for life.

you can imagine them growing golden candlesticks or tigers hanging on by
the tail. These men in spectacles spoke much of a man named Newton,
who was hit by an apple, and who discovered a law. But they could not be
got to see the distinction between a true law, a law of reason, and the mere
fact of apples falling. If the apple hit Newton's nose, Newton's nose hit the
apple. That is a true necessity: because we cannot conceive the one occur-
ring without the other. But we can quite well conceive the apple not falling
on his nose; we can fancy it flying ardently through the air to hit some other
nose, of which it had a more definite dislike. We have always in our fairy
tales kept this sharp distinction between the science of mental relations, in
which there really are laws, and the science of
physical facts, in which there are no laws, but
only weird repetitions. We believe in bodily miracles, but not in mental impossibilities. We believe
that a Bean-stalk climbed up to Heaven; but that
does not at all confuse our convictions on the
philosophical question of how many beans make
five.

Here is the peculiar perfection of tone and
truth in the nursery tales. The man of science
says, "Cut the stalk, and the apple will fall"; but
he says it calmly, as if the one idea really led up to
the other. The witch in the fairy tale says, "Blow
the horn, and the ogre's castle will fall"; but she
does not say it as if it were something in which the
effect obviously arose out of the cause. . . .

Any one can see it who will simply read
"Grimm's Fairy Tales" or the fine collections of
Mr. Andrew Lang. For the pleasure of pedantry I
will call it the Doctrine of Conditional Joy.
Touchstone talked of much virtue in an "if"; ac-
cording to elfin ethics all virtue is in an "if." The

*Chesterton's com-
ments raise the
question of belief.
When we read sto-
ries or watch movies
we are constantly
being asked to sus-
pend our disbelief,
and for the most
part we happily
oblige. Yet when it
comes to something
as simple as belief in
God, there's a ten-
dency to second-
guess and make sure
every aspect is com-
pletely rational and
graspable before
we'll make the leap
of faith.*

note of the fairy utterance always is, "You may live in a palace of gold and sapphire, *if* you do not say the word 'cow' "; or "You may live happily with the King's daughter, *if* you do not show her an onion." The vision always hangs upon a veto. All the dizzy and colossal things conceded depend upon one small thing withheld. All the wild and whirling things that are let loose depend upon one thing that is forbidden. Mr. W. B. Yeats, in his exquisite and piercing elfin poetry, describes the elves as lawless; they plunge in innocent anarchy on the unbridled horses of the air—

*Ride on the crest of the dishevelled tide, And dance upon the mountains like a flame.*

It is a dreadful thing to say that Mr. W. B. Yeats does not understand fairyland. But I do say it. He is an ironical Irishman, full of intellectual reactions. He is not stupid enough to understand fairyland.

Fairies prefer people of the yokel type like myself; people who gape and grin and do as they are told. Mr. Yeats reads into elfland all the righteous insurrection of his own race. But the lawlessness of Ireland is a Christian lawlessness, rounded on reason and justice. The Fenian is rebelling against something he understands only too well; but the true citizen of fairyland is obeying something that he does not understand at all. In the fairy tale an incomprehensible happiness rests upon an incomprehensible condition. A box is opened, and

Chesterton was known for being extremely well-read and had an unusual gift to draw parallels and lessons from a wide variety of published work, as demonstrated here as he floats between some of the best known and loved childhood stories of all time.

Chesterton is reminding us that imagination does not ignore basic scientific principles or practicality—fairy godmothers can still be strict because there are moral standards in their world. However, science and reason don't explain everything in their world, and it would be a mistake to assume they do in ours.

all evils fly out. A word is forgotten, and cities perish. A lamp is lit, and love flies away. A flower is plucked, and human lives are forfeited. An apple is eaten, and the hope of God is gone.

This is the tone of fairy tales, and it is certainly not lawlessness or even liberty, though men under a mean modern tyranny may think it liberty by comparison. People out of Portland Gaol might think Fleet Street free; but closer study will prove that both fairies and journalists are the slaves of duty. Fairy godmothers seem at least as strict as other godmothers.

Cinderella received a coach out of Wonderland and a coachman out of nowhere, but she received a command—which might have come out of Brixton—that she should be back by twelve. Also, she had a glass slipper; and it cannot be a coincidence that glass is so common a substance in folklore. This princess lives in a glass castle, that princess on a glass hill; this one sees all things in a mirror; they may all live in glass houses if they will not throw stones. For this thin glitter of glass everywhere is the expression of the fact that the happiness is bright but brittle, like the substance most easily smashed by a housemaid or a cat. And this fairy-tale sentiment also sank into me and became my sentiment towards the whole world. I felt and feel that life itself is as bright as the diamond, but as brittle as the window-pane; and when the heavens were compared to the terrible crystal I can remember a shudder. I was afraid that God would drop the cosmos with a crash. . . .

Well, I left the fairy tales lying on the floor of the nursery, and I have not found any books so sensible since. I left the nurse guardian of tradition and democracy, and I have not found any modern type so sanely radical or so sanely conservative. But the matter for important comment was here: that when I first went out into the men-

Sometimes life is as "bright as a diamond" or as "brittle as a window-pane" depending on your perspective, but just because you can look at something and see it two different ways does not mean that you should make the mistake of identifying something good as evil or evil as good.

tal atmosphere of the modern world, I found that the modern world was positively opposed on two points to my nurse and to the nursery tales. It has taken me a long time to find out that the modern world is wrong and my nurse was right.

# VITAL STATS

**WHEN AND WHERE:** A Swiss Protestant theologian, Karl Barth was considered a giant in the history of Christian thought. He initiated what became the dominant movement in Protestant theology throughout the twentieth century to the present day.

**STYLE:** Karl Barth's style is intelligent and organized. With a tone of excitement and urgency, he raises a battle cry and a call to arms for Christians to pray for our present world and the fulfillment of God's eternal plans.

**NOTEWORTHY ACCOMPLISHMENTS:** He helped to found the "Confessing Church" in Nazi Germany. This group of ministers met secretly and emerged calling themselves the Protestant Christian Church of Germany. They stood in direct opposition to Hitler's Nazi reign. In 1935 when he refused to take the oath of allegiance to Adolf Hitler, he was retired from his position at the University of Bonn and deported to Switzerland.

**TIMELESS WISDOM:** "The Gospel is not a truth among other truths. Rather, it sets a question mark against all truths." Karl Barth's life inspires us to dig deep into Scripture to know God better and to effectively influence our world for the truth of Christ's saving power.

**KARL BARTH** 1886–1968

Ever wonder what kind of courage it would have taken to stand up and oppose Hitler? Meet someone who did just that: Karl Barth.

Many consider Barth (pronounced "Bart") to be the greatest Protestant theologian since the Reformation. Whether this is true or not, Barth led the way for the renaissance of theology that took place between 1920 and 1950.

He was a professor of theology in Germany just as Hitler was rising to power. He opposed the Hitler regime and instead supported church-sponsored movements against national socialism. During the Second World War, Barth held strong to his convictions and made sure the Nazis knew where he stood. He was ultimately expelled from Bonn, Germany, and returned to Switzerland where he remained until he retired in 1962.

He disliked the fact that the religious philosophy of his day was having a great influence on theology. Barth believed that liberal theology had caused Christianity to accommodate the modern culture, so he did everything he could to move it back toward the principles of the Reformation and the teachings of Scripture. In his writings, he emphasized that the Christian message and the message of the world were indeed different, and they should remain so.

His views became known as neo-orthodoxy and crisis theology, and focused on human sinfulness, God's limitless power (or transcendence), and our inability to know God apart from his revelation of himself through Jesus.

His speaking and writing were a great strength to the people during the war. But in the years that followed, many came to criticize various points of his theology. One controversial view Barth held is that the Bible is not the actual revelation of God but is merely the record of God's revelation; he believed that God's only revelation of himself was in the person of Jesus Christ.

Whether you agree with Barth's stance on these essential issues or not, there's no doubt he is an important figure in recent theological history. For that reason he is a valuable part of this compilation of classic writers. The following excerpt gives a glimpse of his thoughts regarding prayer and the Kingdom of God. Spend some time letting your brain grasp his meaning, and be challenged by the courage he showed in standing up for his beliefs despite great personal risk.

*Dave*

# KARL BARTH
Excerpted from *Prayer and Preaching*[21]

## I. PRAYER IN THE REFORMATION

### *An Intro to Prayer*

Jesus Christ not only told us to pray: in the 'Our Father' he also showed us how to pray, and we should do well to keep to this rule. There must be feeling in prayer, as Calvin says, but feeling must not be an excuse for the mind to wander. The extempore prayers with which Calvin used to end his sermons are remarkable for their stately uniformity; he never indulged in unrestrained outpourings of words. The same elements are always present: adoration of the majesty of God and of the Holy Spirit, but they are not stock phrases.

*Following a brief introduction into the subject of purposeful prayer, Barth examines the Model Prayer or, as some may know it, "The Lord's Prayer."*

## III. THE INTERPRETATION OF THE LORD'S PRAYER ACCORDING TO THE REFORMERS

### 4. THY KINGDOM COME

We have to go somewhat farther than the Reformers, who failed, here as elsewhere, to perceive the eschatological character of that reality which is the Kingdom of God? (I.e., that the Kingdom comes with the end of the world as we know it.) We shall, therefore, give a slightly amended version of their teaching.

The Kingdom of God, in the New Testament, is the life and purpose of the world in accordance

*Reformers? Eschatology? Kingdom of God? In this section, Barth is simply establishing that the Kingdom of God will see its ultimate fulfillment in the end times when sin is defeated once and for all. God's followers will be part of a whole new heaven and earth.*

with the intentions of the Creator; it is the effective and appointed defence against the inevitable consequence of sin, against the mortal danger, the annihilation which lay in wait for the world because it is merely a creature. The Kingdom of God is the final victory over sin; it is the reconciliation of the world with God [II Corinthians 5:19]. And the consequence of that reconciliation is a new world, a new age, a new heaven and a new earth, which are new because they have entered into and are enfolded by the peace of God.

The Kingdom of God is the righteousness of God, the Creator and the Lord who justifies and triumphs. The destiny and purpose of the world is the coming of the Kingdom : 'thy Kingdom come.' Clearly we are once more confronted with a consummation which infinitely exceeds our powers, since all we are and all we can do, even in the most favourable conditions, is threatened by the same danger. We ourselves are in need of that deliverance, that victory, that reconciliation, that renewal. The coming of the Kingdom is in no sense dependent on our power; we are no more able to assist its coming than is creation itself, which is the image of what we are and can do. But it is for us an object of prayer. God alone, who created the world, can bring about its completion in that act of fulfilment in which he vindicates himself and his cross. The Kingdom means the peace and righteousness of the world brought to perfection, and this can only come to pass by the work of God. We must therefore pray that his Kingdom may come and that he may cause the bell to sound the hour of crisis.

But saying to God 'Thy Kingdom come' presupposes that he who prays thus has some knowledge of that Kingdom, that life, that righteousness, that newness, that reconciliation; that these things are not without meaning for him. He

*Barth's words sound like a battle cry of sorts. Imagine all God's glory and power working throughout time to bring us back into a healed relationship with himself. What an eternity to anticipate! What a role we are invited to take in praying "Thy Kingdom come."*

must know also that wherever this prayer is offered the Kingdom has already come.

Once again we are in the amazing position of those who pray 'Our Father' in the fellowship of Jesus Christ and those who are his. *Thy Kingdom come* is equivalent to 'Thy Kingdom is already come; thou hast established it in our midst.' 'The Kingdom of God is among you' [Luke 17:21]. *Thou, God the Father, hast accomplished all things in Jesus Christ; in him thou hast reconciled the world to thyself!*

St Paul does not speak of this reconciliation as a future event. He says 'He **has** reconciled'; it is done. *In Jesus Christ thou hast abolished sin and all its consequences; thou hast destroyed all alien and hostile powers.* 'I saw Satan like lightning fall from heaven' [Luke 10:18]. *Thou hast removed the mortal peril which threatened our lives. Thou, O God, in Jesus Christ didst become the new man who will never die. It is done. In him thy Kingdom has appeared in this world, in all the depth and height of its glory, undiminished and unconcealed.*

> The references to God's Kingdom having already come speak of those who have accepted salvation through Jesus Christ. Jesus' life and death in our place ushered in God's Kingdom, which is now living and active in his followers.

In Jesus Christ the world has reached its end and its goal. Thus, the last judgment and the resurrection of the dead have already been wrought in him; this is not only an event to be awaited, it is already behind us. When the Church speaks of Jesus Christ, when she proclaims his word, when she believes the Gospel and makes it known to the heathen, and when she prays to God, she looks back to her Lord who is already come. She calls to mind Christmas, Good Friday, Easter and Pentecost. These are not just some historical events to which we may attach a religious significance (with the private conviction that in itself this is of no importance). On the contrary, this is everything that has ever happened and is behind us. We proclaim the Word made flesh and the Kingdom of God which has come. The Church is not and cannot be insistent if she does not rejoice, if she is in doubt. A sorrowful and gloomy Church is not the Church! For the Church is built on him who was made flesh, who came to say the last word (not the last but one). This last word has already been uttered and on it our life depends; nothing in it can be changed. The age which began with Christmas and Easter cannot be reversed.

What does this mean when we truly understand it and live by it? It means that we have all the more reason to pray: *Thy Kingdom come!* There is no contradiction here, and one for whom these things are true is well aware of it; that is why he prays.

It means also that God's great initiative on behalf of man, which began at Christmas and Easter and Pentecost, must be resumed so that it may not be simply something that is past and behind us; for we do not live by looking backwards only, but by looking forward also. It must come, the future must bear the stamp of the past, our past must become our future, and the Lord who has come must come again.

### Our Role as Pray-ers

We pray for the removal of the covering which now conceals all things, as a cloth covers a table; the table is underneath though you cannot see it, but the cloth has only to be removed for the table to be seen. We pray that the covering which still veils the reality of the Kingdom may be removed, so that the reality of all those things which have already been changed in Jesus Christ may be seen. Here is the profoundest depth of God's truth, which immeasurably surpasses all else. Our private lives and the lives of our families, the life of the Churches, political events–these are the veil behind which lies reality. As yet we do not see face to face, but only dim reflections as in a mirror. We cannot be sure where we stand when we read the papers, not even the religious papers. So that we may see what truly is, 'thy Kingdom' must come, Jesus Christ must become visible, as he was at Easter, as he showed himself to his apostles. He will be, he is even now, head of the new mankind of the new world. We know this, but as yet we do not see it; we are waiting to see it; we walk by faith, not yet by sight.

May the radiance of God, manifested in Jesus Christ, in his life, his death, and his resurrection, shine upon us, on our whole life and on all things! May the secret of earthly life be revealed, that secret which has already been revealed though as yet we do not see it–hence the anxiety, the cares, the false ideas and the despairs in which we live! We do not understand, and we pray that it may be granted to us to see and understand. . . .

Christians have a job to do. Most of the world continues to be blinded to God's truth. However, at stake are the souls of every human who hasn't yet accepted Jesus' salvation. The prayers of those who know the truth remove the "veil" covering the eyes of the blinded.

### Hope for Here and Now

When we pray, may it be granted to us also to see, even now, at least the first signs of that new age and of that victory which is already won; may the dawn of the universal day enable us to see ourselves and others, and the incidents of our history, in the light of that which is to come. This total revelation, this apokalypsis [I Peter 1:13], will be given to us. May our faith in him who has come be made alive! This can only come to pass if faith is founded on what has happened in the past and looks towards what is to come, which will reveal the universality of what he has accomplished. May it be granted to us to live in that hope. It is not possible to say: 'Thy Kingdom come!' if we are without hope for our own time, for today and tomorrow. The great Future with a capital F is also a future with a small f. This is enough to make us realize, at least in part, how totally inadequate is everything we do in this present time; it brings home to us the triviality of so many of the conflicts in which we are engaged, especially our private, psychological conflicts which, ultimately, are quite unnecessary. But to understand this, we must be able to see the Kingdom which is to come; psychologists cannot help us. One day the sun will rise and full knowledge will be ours. We have only to wait till Easter becomes actual for all the world; then we shall have no more need of psychologists because there will be perfect health. . . . When there is life, there are no more psychological problems.

We pray that it may be granted to us to see the futility of this tragic sense, which befits pagans but not Christians; that we may live in serenity, with good will, and in charity which constrains no one but has the power to attract everyone in some measure. . . .

Happily, in the Kingdom of God there will be no more need of the Church, for Jesus Christ will have completed what he has begun. We must still pray to God because his cause is at stake. His commandments constantly remind us of his patience towards us. During this anxious time of his long-suffering, which we must endure before the Kingdom comes, how necessary it is that God should utter his word and sound the warning bell! Indeed, the end must come! May God fulfil his promises and may we lay hold of them as the promises of God. *Thy Kingdom come—this Kingdom that has come already! Such is our prayer*—simple, constant and very near to him.

> Again, here's Barth's tone of a call to arms. Will we be willing to "sound the warning bell!" to our generation who needs to know God's Kingdom is coming?

# VITAL STATS

**WHEN AND WHERE:** A. W. Tozer became a pastor when he was twenty-two years old. He spent most of his career at Southside Alliance Church in Chicago, Illinois, where he served for thirty-one years.

**STYLE:** A. W. Tozer was a man of prayer who wholeheartedly strove to make worship a major part of his everyday life. It has been said that he spent more time on his knees than at his desk. In addition to his lifelong love of prayer, he was also very fond of words. His sermons and published pieces are filled with beautifully written sentences that go way beyond mere thoughts haphazardly thrown out for review . . . they are carefully, creatively constructed reflections of the charm, wit, and authenticity that made him famous. The man was a creative spiritual genius!

**NOTEWORTHY ACCOMPLISHMENTS:** The epitaph on his tombstone in Akron, Ohio, sums it up best: "A man of God." His very real, authentic faith was indeed his greatest accomplishment and contribution to the world. Though he didn't have a formal theological education, he was a marvelous pastor and served as editor of *Alliance Life*, the Christian and Missionary Alliance's denominational newsletter. He also authored more than forty books, the two most famous being *The Knowledge of the Holy* and *The Pursuit of God*.

**TIMELESS WISDOM:** Don't settle for a mediocre Christian life when you could have something so much more vibrant and alive. An authentic, active relationship with Christ takes work, but the return on the investment of time and self is more than you could ever imagine.

Ever wonder what all God is planning for your life? Wonder what it'd be like to be so connected to him that you can sense his will and know instinctively what he's saying to you? Whether you're a seasoned Christian or a spiritual newbie, it can still amaze you every day that God wants that level of closeness with you. Check out one man's example.

A. W. TOZER 1897–1963

Aiden Wilson Tozer dedicated his life to knowing Christ in an intensely personal way. He spent untold amounts of time on his knees in prayer and developed a strong and intimate connection with the Lord—such a strong connection, in fact, that he reached a point of consistently blocking out every care and distraction that threatened to interfere with their daily time together. As a result, spiritual maturity, passion, and excitement marked his character—by-products of knowing God. And everything Tozer taught was a direct result of his time alone with Christ.

He used God's direction, wisdom, and power supplied during those extended prayer times in his sermons, books, articles, and conversations. As a teacher, Tozer influenced vast numbers during his forty-four-year ministry with the Christian and Missionary Alliance. During thirty-one of those years, Tozer served as pastor at Chicago's Southside Alliance Church—definitely not afraid of long-term commitment!

His books *The Knowledge of the Holy* and *The Pursuit of God* are spiritual classics. The excerpt below is from the latter. Amazingly, Tozer wrote the entire first draft by pulling a crazy all-nighter on a train bound for Texas from Chicago. He said the words just kept coming to him as fast as he could get them down on paper.

Knowing he was tired and train-lagged makes the depth of *The Pursuit of God* even more impressive. And it proves how heartfelt the experience really was for him. The book's basic theme is the irony of being pursued by God while sincerely pursuing him as well. Tozer raises deep heart issues that draw the reader into serious reflection and honest self-disclosure before God.

The following excerpt is from the first chapter, "Following Hard after God." It sets the tone for the rest of the book by revealing what it means to pursue God and how being a "seeker" isn't a name reserved for people who haven't yet entered into a saving relationship with Christ.

It's so easy to get caught up in doing, doing, doing. But intimacy with God comes through investing time in an active, growing relationship and an intentionally deeper soul connection with the Lord. If you're not sure what that means, you're in for a treat with this excerpt.

*The Pursuit of God* is one of those books that will rock your world and change your life. Allow your understanding to grow to a deeper level in hot pursuit of Christ, our Lover. You will be hard-pressed to find a book more meaningful in your own relationship with Christ!

*Janella*

## A. W. TOZER
Excerpted from *The Pursuit of God*[22]

## CHAPTER 1: FOLLOWING HARD AFTER GOD

*My soul followeth hard after thee: thy right hand upholdeth me.*

Psalm 63:8

Christian theology teaches the doctrine of prevenient grace, which briefly stated means this, that before a man can seek God, God must first have sought the man.

Before a sinful man can think a right thought of God, there must have been a work of enlightenment done within him; imperfect it may be, but a true work nonetheless, and the secret cause of all desiring and seeking and praying which may follow.

We pursue God because, and only because, He has first put an urge within us that spurs us to the pursuit. "No man can come to me," said our Lord, "except the Father which hath sent me draw him," and it is by this very prevenient *drawing* that God takes from us every vestige of credit for the act of coming. The impulse to pursue God originates with God, but the outworking of that impulse is our following hard after Him; and all the time we are pursuing Him we are already in His hand: "Thy right hand upholdeth me."

In this divine "upholding" and human "following" there is no contradiction. All is of God, for as von Hügel teaches, *God is always previous.* In practice, however, (that is, where God's previous working meets man's present response) man must pursue God. On our part there must be positive reciprocation if this secret drawing of God is to eventuate in identifiable experience of the Divine. In the warm language of personal feeling this is stated in the Forty-second Psalm: "As the hart panteth after the water brooks, so panteth my soul after thee, O God. My soul thirsteth for God, for the living God: when shall I come and appear before God?" This is deep calling unto deep, and the longing heart will understand it.

The doctrine of justification by faith—a Biblical truth, and a blessed relief from sterile legalism and unavailing self-effort—has in our time fallen into evil company and been interpreted by many in such manner as actually to bar men from the knowledge of God. The whole transaction of religious conversion has been made mechanical and spiritless. Faith may now be exercised without a jar to the moral life and without embarrassment to the Adamic ego. Christ may be "received" without creating any special love for Him in the soul of the receiver. The man is "saved," but he is not hungry nor thirsty after God. In fact he is specifically taught to be satisfied and encouraged to be content with little. . . .

> Mindlessly repeating a bunch of religious rhetoric that leads to no significant change of heart, action, or thought can hardly be considered a "salvation experience!"

### God Is a Person and Therefore Personal

God is a Person, and in the deep of His mighty nature He thinks, wills, enjoys, feels, loves, desires and suffers as any other person may. In making Himself known to us He stays by the familiar pattern of personality. He communicates with us through the avenues of our minds, our wills and our emotions. The continuous and unembarrassed interchange of love and thought between God and the soul of the redeemed man is the throbbing heart of New Testament religion. . . .

You and I are in little (our sins excepted) what God is in large. Being made in His image we have within us the capacity to know Him. In our sins we lack only the power. The moment the Spirit has quickened us to life in regeneration our whole being senses its kinship to God and leaps up in joyous recognition. That is the heavenly birth without which we cannot see the Kingdom of God. It is, however, not an end but an inception, for now begins the glorious pursuit, the heart's happy exploration of the infinite riches of the Godhead. That is where we begin, I say, but where we stop no man has yet discovered, for there is in the awful and mysterious depths of the Triune God neither limit nor end.

> *Shoreless Ocean, who can sound Thee?*
> *Thine own eternity is round Thee,*
> *Majesty divine!*

To have found God and still to pursue Him is the soul's paradox of love, scorned indeed by the too-easily-satisfied religionist, but justified in happy experience by the children of the burning heart.

St. Bernard stated this holy paradox in a musical quatrain that will be instantly understood by every worshipping soul:

Let this be the beautiful reality of our generation: "children of the burning heart" pursuing him through the "soul's paradox of love."

> *We taste Thee, O Thou Living Bread,*
> *And long to feast upon Thee still:*
> *We drink of Thee, the Fountainhead*
> *And thirst our souls from Thee to fill.*

### Longing for God

Come near to the holy men and women of the past and you will soon feel the heat of their desire after God. They mourned for Him, they prayed and wrestled and sought for Him day and night, in season and out, and when they had found Him the finding was all the sweeter for the long seeking. Moses used the fact that he knew God as an argument for knowing Him better. "Now, therefore, I pray thee, if I have found grace in thy sight, show me now thy way, that I may know thee, that I may find grace in thy sight"; and from there he rose to make the daring request, "I beseech thee, show me thy glory." God was frankly pleased by this display of ardor, and the next day called Mo-

God loves it when we passionately pursue him!

ses into the mount, and there in solemn procession made all His glory pass before him.

David's life was a torrent of spiritual desire, and his psalms ring with the cry of the seeker and the glad shout of the finder. Paul confessed the mainspring of his life to be his burning desire after Christ. "That I may know Him," was the goal of his heart, and to this he sacrificed everything. "Yea doubtless, and I count all things but loss for the excellency of the knowledge of Christ Jesus my Lord: for whom I have suffered the loss of all things, and do count them but refuse, that I may win Christ."

*If you want to seek God, but don't really know what that looks like or where to start, read through the Psalms. Pray them out loud. Make them your own. David's a great teacher when it comes to the pursuit of God.*

Hymnody is sweet with the longing after God, the God whom, while the singer seeks, he knows he has already found. "His track I see and I'll pursue," sang our fathers only a short generation ago, but that song is heard no more in the great congregation. How tragic that we in this dark day have had our seeking done for us by our teachers. Everything is made to center upon the initial act of "accepting" Christ (a term, incidentally, which is not found in the Bible) and we are not expected thereafter to crave any further revelation of God to our souls. We have been snared in the coils of a spurious logic which insists that if we have found Him we need no more seek Him. This is set before us as the last word in orthodoxy, and it is taken for granted that no Bible-taught Christian ever believed otherwise. Thus the whole testimony of the worshipping, seeking, singing Church on that subject is crisply set aside. The experiential heart-theology of a grand army of fragrant saints is rejected in favor of a smug interpretation of Scripture which would certainly have sounded strange to an Augustine, a Rutherford or a Branierd.

In the midst of this great chill there are some, I rejoice to acknowledge, who will not be content with shallow logic. They will admit the force of the argument, and then turn away with tears to hunt some lonely place and

Tozer is asserting
here that worship
is an experiential
matter of the heart,
and that "seekers"
are not merely the
unsaved. We should
all be "seekers" who
continue to grow
closer to God.

pray, "O God, show me thy glory." They want to taste, to touch with their hearts, to see with their inner eyes the wonder that is God.

I want deliberately to encourage this mighty longing after God. The lack of it has brought us to our present low estate. The stiff and wooden quality about our religious lives is a result of our lack of holy desire. Complacency is a deadly foe of all spiritual growth. Acute desire must be present or there will be no manifestation of Christ to His people. He waits to be wanted. Too bad that with many of us He waits so long, so very long, in vain.

## Back to Basics

Every age has its own characteristics. Right now we are in an age of religious complexity. The simplicity which is in Christ is rarely found among us. In its stead are programs, methods, organizations and a world of nervous activities which occupy time and attention but can never satisfy the longing of the heart. The shallowness of our inner experience, the hollowness of our worship, and that servile imitation of the world which marks our promotional methods all testify that we, in this day, know God only imperfectly, and the peace of God scarcely at all.

If we would find God amid all the religious externals we must first determine to find Him, and then proceed in the way of simplicity. Now as always God discovers Himself to "babes" and hides Himself in thick darkness from the wise and the prudent. We must simplify our approach to Him. We must strip down to essentials (and they will be found to be blessedly few). We must put away all effort to impress, and come with the guileless candor of childhood. If we do this, without doubt God will quickly respond.

When religion has said its last word, there is little that we need other than God Himself. The evil habit of seeking *God-and* effectively prevents us from finding God in full revelation. In the "and" lies our great woe. If we omit the "and" we shall soon find God, and in Him we shall find that for which we have all our lives been secretly longing. . . .

When the Lord divided Canaan among the tribes of Israel Levi received no share of the land. God said to him simply, "I am thy part and thine inheritance," and by those words made him richer than all his brethren, richer than all the kings and rajas who have ever lived in the world. And there is a spiritual principle here, a principle still valid for every priest of the Most High God.

*Tozer was known for his own very simple, unfettered personal faith. He practiced what he's preaching here!*

The man who has God for his treasure has all things in One. Many ordinary treasures may be denied him, or if he is allowed to have them, the enjoyment of them will be so tempered that they will never be necessary to his happiness. Or if he must see them go, one after one, he will scarcely feel a sense of loss, for having the Source of all things he has in One all satisfaction, all pleasure, all delight. Whatever he may lose he has actually lost nothing, for he now has it all in One, and he has it purely, legitimately and forever.

*O God, I have tasted Thy goodness, and it has both satisfied me and made me thirsty for more. I am painfully conscious of my need of further grace. I am ashamed of my lack of desire. O God, the Triune God, I want to want Thee; I long to be filled with longing; I thirst to be made more thirsty still. Show me Thy glory, I pray Thee, that so I may know Thee indeed. Begin in mercy a new work of love within me. Say to my soul, "Rise up, my love, my fair one, and come away." Then give me grace to rise and follow Thee up from this misty lowland where I have wandered so long. In Jesus' name, Amen.*

1. Saint Augustine, *Confessions*. Translated by Albert C. Outler (Philadelphia, PA: Westminster Press, 1955), http://www.ccel.org/a/augustine/confessions/confesions.html (accessed August 22, 2005).

2. Julian, *Revelations of Divine Love*. (Grand Rapids, MI: Christian Classics Ethereal Library, 2002), http://www.ccel.org/ccel/julian/revelations.toc.html (accessed September 7, 2005).

3. Thomas à Kempis, *The Imitation of Christ* (Milwaukee: Bruce Publishing Company, 1949), http://www.ccel.org/ccel/kempis/imitation.html (accessed September 7, 2005).

4. Martin Luther, *The Bondage of the Will*. Translated by Henry Cole (Grand Rapids, MI: Wm. B. Eerdmans Publishing, 1931), http://www.truecovenanter.com/truelutheran/luther_bow.html (accessed September 7, 2005).

5. John Calvin, *Calvin's Institutes*. Translated by Henry Beveridge (Grand Rapids, MI: Christian Classics Ethereal Library, 2001), http://www.ccel.org/ccel/calvin/institutes.iv.iii.x.html (accessed September 9, 2005).

6. Prayer of St. Teresa of Ávila, http://www.day1.net/transcript.php?id=435 (Web site is no longer available).

7. St. Teresa of Ávila, *The Way of Perfection*. Translated by E. Allison Peers (Grand Rapids, MI: Christian Classics Ethereal Library, 2000), http://www.ccel.org/t/teresa/way (accessed August 22, 2005).

8. Brother Lawrence, *The Practice of the Presence of God* (Grand Rapids, MI: Christian Classics Ethereal Library, 2001), http://www.ccel.org/ccel/lawrence/practice.htm (accessed August 22, 2005).

9. John Bunyan, *The Pilgrim's Progress* (Grand Rapids, MI: Baker Book House, 1984), 170–178. See also http://www.ccel.org/b/bunyan/pilgrims_progress/title.html.

10. Madame Guyon, *A Short and Easy Method of Prayer* (Grand Rapids, MI: Christian Classics Ethereal Library, 2002), http://www.ccel.org/ccel/guyon/prayer.html (accessed September 9, 2005).

11. William Law, *A Serious Call to a Devout and Holy Life* (London: J. M. Dent and Sons, 1967), 1–7. See also http://www.ccel.org/ccel/law/serious_call.html.

12. Charles Wesley, "Awake, Thou That Sleepest," http://gbgm-umc.org/umhistory/wesley/sermons/serm-003.stm (accessed September 7, 2005).

13. George Whitefield, "Christ the Believer's Husband," in *Whitefield's Sermons* (Grand Rapids, MI: Christian Classics Ethereal Library), http://www.ccel.org/ccel/whitefield/sermons.xiv.html (accessed September 9, 2005).

14. Frederick Douglass, *My Bondage and My Freedom* (Urbana, IL: University of Illinois Press, 1987), 103–108. See also http://etext.lib.virginia.edu/toc/modeng/public/DouMybo.html.

15. Andrew Murray, *Absolute Surrender and Other Addresses* (Chicago: Moody Press, 1895), http://www.ccel.org/ccel/murray/surrender.iii.html (accessed September 9, 2005).

16. Hannah Whitall Smith, *The God of All Comfort* (Chicago: Moody Press, 1956), 32–34, 36–38, 41–45. See also http://ccel.org/ccel/smith_hw/comfort.III.html.

17. C. H. Spurgeon, *All of Grace,* http://www.ccel.org/s/spurgeon/grace (accessed September 9, 2005).

18. Dorsett, Lyle W., *A Passion for Souls: The Life of D. L. Moody* (Chicago: Moody Press, 1997).

19. Moody, D. L., *The Overcoming Life* (Chicago: Moody Press, 1995), 79–88.

20. G. K. Chesterton, *Orthodoxy* (Garden City, NY: Doubleday and Company, Inc., 1936), 46, 49–51, 55–56, 58. See also http://www.ccel.org/ccel/chesterton/orthodoxy.html.

21. Karl Barth, *Prayer and Preaching,* http://www.worldinvisible.com/library/barth/prayerpreaching/prayerpreaching.c.htm (accessed September 9, 2005).

22. A.W. Tozer, *The Pursuit of God* (Harrisburg, PA: Christian Publications, 1948), 11–20. See also http://calvarychapel.com/library/Tozer-AW/PursuitOfGod/0.htm.

■ Get a job
■ Pay the rent
■ Find a church
■ Go to the gym
■ Call Mom and Dad
■ Pick up dry cleaning
■ Return videos

You want a life of purpose and meaning.
You've got the passion.
But who's got the time?

From defining your relationships and
managing your money and career to
strengthening your faith and understanding the culture around you, *Everything Twentys* will help you make the
most of the best decade of your life!

Pick up a copy of *Everything Twentys* today!
Available now at a bookstore near you.

# what the heck am I going to do with my life?

## IT'S A QUESTION THAT JUST WON'T GO AWAY.

Maybe you just graduated with a degree in business only to discover that you hate business. You like the idea of being a teacher *except* for the students, and you love public service *except* for the people.

That's when it hits you—you've spent the last four years pursuing what you thought was the career of your dreams, and now you're wondering, *Is this it?*

Well, guess what—you're not alone.

The good news is it's *never* too late to pursue your passion. You can still discover that thing you were created to do. You can go back to school, launch a new business, change professions—whatever you'd like. This book is designed to accompany you on that journey.

+ + +     + + +     + + +     + + +     + + +

**SO GO AHEAD.** /// Ask the question and be daring enough to find the answer.
**BE BRAVE.** /// You never know what kind of opportunities might be around the next corner.

## AVAILABLE NOW AT A BOOKSTORE NEAR YOU!